Historic Haunts
of
Winchester

Historic Haunts
of Winchester
A Ghostly Trip Through the Past

Mac Rutherford

Haunted America

Published by Haunted America
A Division of The History Press
Charleston, SC 29403
www.historypress.net

Cover image: *A Night on the Battlefield.* Tillie over a wounded solider. *A drawing by M.K. Kellogg, courtesy of the Handley Regional Library Archives.*
All images courtesy of Sally Coates unless otherwise noted.

First published 2007
Second printing 2010
Third printing 2012
Fourth printing 2013

ISBN 978-1-5402-1784-4

Library of Congress Cataloging-in-Publication Data

Rutherford, Mac.
Historic haunts of Winchester : a ghostly trip through the past / Mac
Rutherford.
p. cm.
ISBN-13: 978-1-59629-297-0 (alk. paper)
1. Ghosts--Virginia--Winchester. 2. Haunted places--Virginia--Winchester.
3. Winchester (Va.)--History. I. Title.
BF1472.U6R88 2007
133.109755'991--dc22
2007027251

Notice: The information in this book is true and complete to the best of our knowledge. It is offered without guarantee on the part of the author or The History Press. The author and The History Press disclaim all liability in connection with the use of this book.

Contents

CONTENTS

Foreword

Welcome to Old Town Winchester, the heart and hub of Winchester-Frederick County, Virginia!

As the marketplace and center of cultural and governmental activities for over 250 years, Old Town Winchester embodies the community's past, present and future spirit. Retail shops, galleries, restaurants and cafés, museums and churches welcome visitors and residents alike with warm, congenial hospitality. A quaint pedestrian mall offers a relaxing atmosphere away from big-box stores and vehicular traffic.

Lining the streets of the forty-five-block historic district are hundreds of antebellum and late nineteenth-century buildings. Constructed of limestone, brick and wood, they speak volumes in terms of the area's

With lots of unique shops and restaurants, visitors always find something fun to do on the Loudoun Street walking mall.

architectural history. Within the walls of these wonderful old structures, there are fascinating stories to be told.

In this book, local historian Mac Rutherford presents some of the stories that are unique to Old Town Winchester and its buildings. Mac's specialty is ghosts. His subjects are, quite naturally, inhabitants of Old Town.

As a preservationist and storyteller, Mac carefully weaves legendary lore into each of his tales. His personal appreciation of local history, unique marketing skills and friendly personality combine to make each of his stories a delightful journey into the past. When you finish reading the book, you'll want to take his Historic Haunts of Winchester Walking Tour so that you too can experience Old Town Winchester's hospitality.

Sally C. Coates
May 12, 2007

Winchester, Virginia

Winchester is the oldest town established west of the Blue Ridge Mountains. Spirits or ghosts, as they are commonly known, abound. In their strange world, heroes from the War for Southern Independence rub shoulders with heroes from the American Revolution. Patsy Cline continues to move about town, much as she did before she became a star, and Native Americans are still seen in Indian Alley.

They share their spirit world with us, but we the living cannot comprehend it. We can hear them, feel them and there are times when some of us can even see them, but we have no understanding. No one from the living world has ever been to the spirit world and returned to tell about it.

Their world remains in a shroud of mystery, a world that some of us believe exists and others refuse to accept. And so it will remain until someone finds a way into their world and comes back again.

The Winchester area was home to Native Americans long before Europeans crossed the Atlantic Ocean. For centuries, the entire Shenandoah Valley was a vast hunting ground for Native American tribes such as the Senedoes, Iroquois and Shawnee.

In 1670, Virginia Governor William Berkeley sent John Lederer to explore uncharted lands to the west. Lederer, the first European to cross the Blue Ridge Mountains and see the Shenandoah Valley, journeyed three times into the area.

By the early 1700s, Germans and Scots-Irish from Pennsylvania and English from Williamsburg found their way to the Shenandoah Valley.

Thomas Lord Fairfax, who owned over five million acres of Virginia soil, gave land grants to the Germans, Scots-Irish and English. With the help of James Wood, George Washington and Daniel Morgan, Winchester became a town in 1752.

This majestic statue of George Washington as a young surveyor, situated in the courtyard of George Washington's Office Museum, is a "must-see" for all visitors.

Washington first came to Winchester as a sixteen-year-old surveyor, hired by Lord Fairfax. He later commanded the local militia force in Winchester during the French and Indian War.

These hardy men and women left their blood, tears and sweat to settle a new land. Perhaps, they left their spirits as well.

Introduction
As the Sun Drops Slowly

In the western sky, the shadows grow long in the old town of Winchester, Virginia, shrouding the city in an eerie mystery. It is a mystery that carries the mind into the world of the paranormal where spirits beckon from beyond and a journey to the dark side waits. Perhaps a few thoughts are needed on ghosts and what they are, or what they might be. Do spirits know they are dead? Do they see us, the living? Do they try to communicate with the living world? How do they come to be, and how are they created?

The only thing we know for sure is that we don't know anything about the paranormal world. We have no clue as to what a ghost is or how it is created. All we can do is speculate. Everything we don't know about the spirit world or think we do know is theory. The rank amateur is as qualified to theorize about the spirit world as the experienced paranormal researcher. Neither the amateur nor the experienced researcher has been to the other side!

We will venture some guesses no better, no worse, than others. First, what is a spirit? It is, in our opinion, energy—the mental and physical energy that remains after the body departs from the living world. If we accept the fact that living beings are made up of energy, then the energy theory becomes quite plausible. Once created, energy can never be destroyed; it will always exist. Therefore, the energy left behind becomes a spirit, a ghost. But, the remaining energy needs psychic power from the living to grow into a spirit to be seen, heard or felt. By drawing vigor from the living, the spirit is able to move about and conduct business of its own.

It is our belief that ghosts remain in their own time period and are not much concerned about our world and us. A ghost who lived in Winchester in 1861 is far more concerned about the gathering war storm. When a spirit does take the time to see our world, how strange it must seem. They surely realize that the beings of today have not learned very much from the past.

What are cold spots? It is generally believed that a cold spot is a spirit's way of announcing its presence. The best explanation for this phenomenon came from a thirteen-year-old girl who advanced the theory that perhaps a cold spot occurs because the ghost is drawing energy and heat from the living.

Another theory relative to ghosts is that they are spirits who refuse to go to the other side. They are still lingering with us because they have unfinished business.

Look! The sun is sinking in the west; the shadows are becoming long. The time has come to explore the world of ghosts. Come now, if you dare. Come and read about the dark side of Winchester. Read with an open mind, and perhaps, when you have finished, you may have an answer to questions that have haunted mankind since the dawn of time.

Confederate in the Window

25 West Piccadilly Street (Formerly Colonial Art and Craft)

COLONEL GEORGE S. PATTON

It happened late one afternoon during the 1980s. Colonel George Smith Patton, Twenty-second Virginia, CSA, appeared from nowhere. My friend Mark, an artist, and I were traveling west on Piccadilly Street. We passed the Colonial Art and Craft store, an impressive building on the south side of the street. It had been the home of Phillip Williams, a Winchester lawyer, during the War for Southern Independence.

As we passed the store, Mark became excited and shouted in surprise, "Look at that! I've never seen a reenactor who looks so real. Did you see him standing there and looking out the window?"

Of course I didn't see him; I was driving.

"Stop, I've got to sketch that guy," Mark said.

After turning the corner and parking, Mark collected his bag of pens and sketchpads and was off. When he reached the Colonial Art and Craft store, there was no reenactor looking out the window. He asked for the reenactor and was told, "We don't have a reenactor here, never have."

Mark protested, "I saw what I saw. He had a full beard; he was wearing a Confederate officer's uniform, and he was gazing north. His eyes, they were terrible, like something was wrong."

The store manager then explained that people frequently came in to tell him about the Confederate officer they saw standing at the window. While listening to Mark and the store manager, it became very clear to me that the room was cold. It was too cold for a warm day. Also, there was something that made the hair on the back of my neck stand up.

Colonel Patton, grandfather of World War II hero George Smith Patton who commanded the Third U.S. Army during the push into Germany

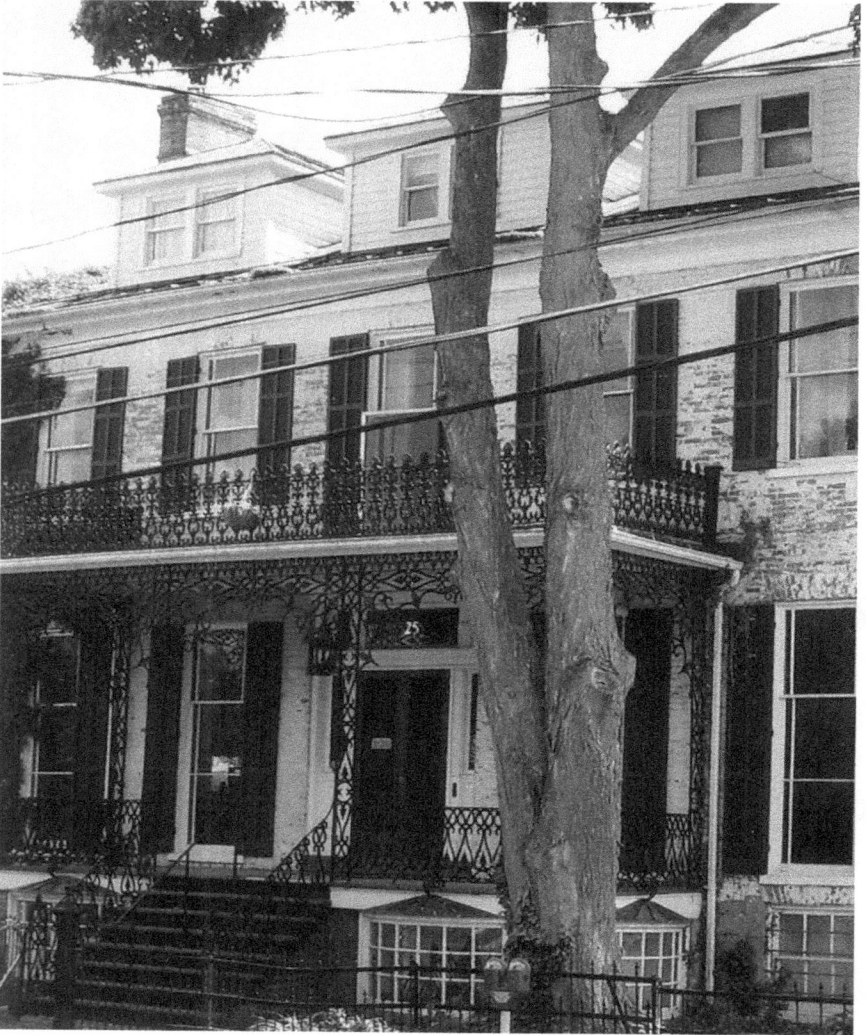

This fine old home, located at 25 West Piccadilly Street, will forever be known as the Philip Williams House. For many years, the Colonial Art and Craft Shop was located in the building.

following D-Day, died in the house from wounds suffered during the Third Battle of Winchester, September 19, 1864.

Colonel George S. Patton and his brother, Colonel Waller Tazewell Patton of the Seventh Virginia, were cousins to Phillip Williams. After

George S. Patton was wounded in the leg during the Third Battle of Winchester, he was taken to his cousin's home. When the doctor came to see Patton, he explained the options—amputate the leg or die. Legend has it that upon hearing this grave outlook, Patton reached for his pistol on the nightstand and pointed it at the doctor, proclaiming, "No one is going to cut my leg off. I'm going to live to dance on this leg again."

We know the leg was not taken off and the colonel died in short order. The injury that resulted in Patton's death was not his first serious wound. He had encountered repeated wounds during battles—for he was always where the action was thick and heavy.

Once, after recovering from a wound at his home in Lexington, Patton was mounting his horse to return to the Twenty-second Virginia when his wife gave him a twenty-dollar gold piece. She told him, "You're going to be wounded and this money will save your life."

As predicted, during the next battle involving the Twenty-second Virginia, Patton was hit in the chest. Thinking the wound was fatal, the doctors placed him outside, under a tree. After the action had ended, the doctors decided to have a look at the colonel. To their surprise, he was still alive. The bullet had hit the gold piece that Patton was carrying in his breast pocket.

But by the Third Battle of Winchester, luck had turned its back on the colonel. It was not long after his death that reports began circulating about a ghostly apparition standing in the window.

Currently, the Phillip Williams house is home to a bank. One of the employees, who works in the room where Patton died, has eerie feelings:

> *It's spooky in here. It's always cold and I can never get over the feeling that someone else is here. Someone I can't see. It feels as though someone is behind me at the window. I look, but I can't see anyone, yet I know someone is there. I have seen something like a shadow walking toward the window, but I've always figured my mind was playing a trick.*

George S. Patton shares a grave with his brother, Waller Tazewell Patton, in the Stonewall section of Winchester's Mount Hebron Cemetery. Although the Patton brothers have been dead for more than 140 years, they still cause a ghostly sensation in Winchester. Visitors in the Stonewall Cemetery often see a small man in a military coat and hat in front of the Patton grave. The man is described as powerful for his size. Upon approaching the man at the grave, he will glance up, revealing a full black beard. In a split second, the man is no longer there.

The Patton brothers—George S. and W. Tazewell—are buried together in the Stonewall Confederate Cemetery.

For years, a debate has raged: Who is the little man at the Pattons' grave? One Winchester historian advanced the theory that the apparition at the Patton grave is none other than World War II Field Marshal Erwin Rommel. The only basis for this is that, according to Winchester tradition, Rommel was

Turner and Richard Ashby are remembered on this memorial located in the Stonewall Confederate Cemetery.

with a group of German officers who were in Winchester in the early 1930s to study the campaigns of Confederate General T.J. (Stonewall) Jackson.

This is hard to accept. For insight regarding the little man, I took a friend who can communicate with the spirit world to the Patton brothers' grave and asked, "What, if anything, do you see?"

After looking about for a few minutes, she pointed to the Patton grave and said, "In front of that grave there is a small man. A very unusual man, he's strong and powerful for his size. He has a black beard and a passionate love for horses. In fact, he always rides a black or white horse."

Mystery solved! Four graves south of the Patton brothers' is the grave of General Turner Ashby. Described as a very powerful and strong little man with a black beard, Ashby commanded Jackson's cavalry during the 1862 Valley Campaign, and he always rode either a black or white horse. Ashby became a Winchester legend in March 1862. While protecting Jackson's retreating army, he rode down a Yankee soldier, lifted him onto his own horse and used the Yankee as a human shield while making his escape.

The Cork Street Tavern

8 West Cork Street

SPIRITS IN THE TAVERN

The Cork Street Tavern is an inviting place, serving fine food and spirits. Enter and enjoy this cozy restaurant that dates back to 1827, and perhaps you'll encounter one of the spirits who shares this space with the living.

Joel and Anthony opened Cork Street Tavern in 1985, and it wasn't long before they became acquainted with the ghosts—John and Emily—who came with the building. The tavern is divided into two sections—the older part of the building and the newer part. It's in the old section that things go bump in the night. Hosts Joel and Anthony are happy to share stories of ghostly happenings that take place in the tavern.

"I can't remember how it happened," says Joel, "but we weren't open long when we heard a female voice calling 'John.' Since that first time, a lot of things have happened here."

The Cork Street Tavern staff gave the name "Emily" to the female voice, and once Emily started calling John, it didn't take long for the gentleman to make an appearance. Joel was one of the first to see John. "He came in through the front door," said Joel. "He stopped, looked around the room, then walked across the room, and was gone. Since then, several of the staff, servers, and bartenders have seen John make his entrance. It makes the hair on the back of your neck stand up. At first all he did was come in and look around, then walk across the room, but that soon changed."

Research has revealed that the old section of the Cork Street Tavern was built in 1827, and the first owner was a gentleman named John Mann. "It's spooky to know that John Mann built the structure and lived here. We never knew anyone named John lived here," admits Joel.

John Mann was a deeply religious man. He built a church for slaves and free blacks circa 1858. It was named the John Mann Methodist Church. Today the church still carries his name and stands less than two blocks east of the tavern.

Everyone willing to confess to seeing John describes him as "a tall, thin man, dressed in a long black frock coat." But there is more happening at the tavern than just a voice calling "John" and an apparition walking across the room.

Once, when Joel was cooking, all the hamburger buns were suddenly pulled off the bread rack. Joel had to stop cooking and pick the buns up. No sooner had he returned to cooking than the buns were pulled off the rack again. After the fourth time, Joel looked around and politely said, "Will you please leave my hamburger buns alone?" Although the hamburger buns weren't touched again, the dinner rolls were now pulled off the shelf. "I didn't say anything more. I just left the rolls on the floor," said Joel.

Nowadays, when Joel and Anthony interview an applicant for a position at the tavern, they tell the candidate, "We have ghosts. If you work here, sooner or later you will have an experience." And it's a well-heeded warning, for over the past twenty-two years, John and Emily have increased their haunting. Several staffers have reported seeing a woman behind the bar in the old section, but no one has been able to get a close look at her. "She is only seen when no one else is in the room, and when someone comes in, she quickly disappears. We only get a glimpse of her, but we can tell it's a woman," said Joel.

Not very long ago, one of the cooks was making potato skins when he "felt" someone come into the kitchen. Upon looking up, he saw a tall, thin man dressed in black. The man walked to the counter and yanked the wax paper onto which the cook was placing the skins. Every potato skin went flying and landed on the floor!

Another recent happening came late one night, about closing time. One of the waitresses had just finished her shift and was sitting at a table with other staff members. Suddenly, the girl sitting next to her let out a scream as she watched an earring come off the ear of the other girl and float across the room!

At times, a gentleman diner in the old section looks around the room and, with a bewildered look, he asks the folks he's with, "Did you hear someone call my name?" Of course, the gentleman's name is always "John"! Not to be forgotten, female patrons receive their own share of

Spirits continue to play folly in the Cork Street Tavern.

attention. Something that spooks the women is getting locked in the ladies' room. When John or Emily locks a woman in the ladies' room, no manner of pulling and tugging will open the door. Only a male member of the kitchen staff can open the door.

The spirits, John and Emily, also enjoy playing tricks with small oil lights on the tables. There are times when a member of the staff lights the wicks, only to hear someone come from behind and blow them out. On one occasion, the closing bartender blew out the lamps, locked up and walked across the street to her car. When she glanced back toward the tavern, all of the lamps were burning. However, their pranks do not stop here. For whatever reason, Joel and Anthony used to have an old snowshoe on the wall in the old section. No matter how securely the shoe was attached to the wall, several times a day it fell to the floor. Finally, the old snowshoe was moved to the new section of the building—where nothing mysterious ever transpires.

Perhaps the most frequent occurrence is women stumbling as they enter the nonsmoking section of the old side. Every day a woman stumbles, but never falls. My daughter, Tara, has even been a victim of the stumble. One of my friends with "the gift" has sensed that a free black man is sitting at a table near the spot where women stumble. She says that the man does not like women, and he tries to trip them, but in fear, he pulls his foot back to prevent a fall.

The history of the Cork Street Tavern is well recorded, except for during the Prohibition years. During that time, it is almost as though the building did not exist. Research revealed that during those days, it was a speakeasy and brothel. More than once, a local gentleman lost his life while visiting the nightspot. Instead of the deaths being reported, the victims were quickly and quietly buried in the basement.

An interesting thing concerning the basement of the tavern happened during one of my ghost tours. A group of psychics from Baltimore refused to enter the old section because of the death they felt in the basement. "There are people buried down there and their deaths were never reported. They are unsettled spirits who are very unhappy."

Indeed, no one dares go into that part of the tavern's basement…

Stone Soup

107 North Loudoun Street

JEANETTE

In 1764, Miller's Apothecary opened for business at 107 North Loudoun Street. After over two hundred years in business, the Miller family gave up the apothecary, and in 1992 the old building was sold to Debbie. Unaware of what she had purchased, Debbie set about restoring the structure, with the goal of returning it to its 1764 glory.

The night before the grand opening of her business, Stone Soup Gallery, Debbie had a party for several friends. During the night, one of the girls awakened to find a young woman in a Colonial dress standing over her. Thinking it was Debbie, the friend nodded off and went back to sleep. The next morning, she asked Debbie why she was rambling around so late and dressed in such a strange fashion. Debbie responded that she was not up late. In fact, she slept through the night and she did not own such a dress!

Stone Soup opened on schedule, and among the curious browsers was a Winchester lawyer. While in one of the back rooms, the lawyer was startled to feel a very cold breeze pass him. After the first tingling had passed, the lawyer saw a young woman standing near him. She was forming words with her mouth, but no sounds were uttered. Then she faded away, or so it appeared. Thinking she was an employee, the lawyer complimented Debbie on the unique way she fashioned young women in Colonial-style clothing. This time, Debbie realized that perhaps there were others sharing her building. She called a well-known woman who can communicate with spirits on the "other side."

Turns out that the building was bursting with spirits, one of whom, Jeanette, had occupied the building since the late 1700s, when she moved in with the Miller family. As a young woman, Jeanette found herself pregnant by a young man named John Boyd. (John was a name that had been passed down in the Boyd family.) The Boyd family lived in Bunker Hill and conducted business in Winchester, which was about nine miles away.

Jeanette's child, a boy she named Josiah, died when he was six weeks old. He was buried in the basement near one of the fireplaces. Jeanette stays with her baby during the mornings and early afternoons, when "it's too noisy." As a result, most of the Jeanette sightings occur late in the afternoon.

In 2004, Debbie sold the gallery to the owners of the Village Square Restaurant, a thriving business located on the west side of Stone Soup. As the walls of the two buildings are connected, installation of a linking door was fairly easy. Stone Soup was remodeled into a piano bar and the back rooms were converted into dining rooms.

When the new piano bar, V2, opened, Jeanette was there to help greet the new customers.

"She's still here," said co-owner David Smith.

> She has been making her presence known since day one. At first, it was the cold breeze in the back rooms. Then we started seeing her.
>
> At first, it was scary, but now it's no big deal to see or feel her; she grows on you. I've seen her several times, as has most of the staff. Everyone who sees her always describes her in the same way. She's of slight build, has medium light brown hair and wears a long flowing dress. At times, she is a shadowy gray and you can almost see through her. At other times, she is as solid as anyone.

However, Jeanette is not the only spirit in the building. A new spirit has been seen going between the two establishments. "She's a young girl," Smith said, "and she walks back and forth."

Not long ago, during a big party in one of the back rooms, a glass flew off a shelf and shattered on the floor. Later a strange occurrence took place as the staff completed preparations for another large party. The refrigerator was stocked and its door was tightly secured with duct tape. As one of the assistant chefs was finishing up, he heard the duct tape being ripped off the refrigerator door. He glanced up to see it being pulled away.

Additionally, upstairs they have heard the sounds of pacing boots and arguing men.

"I've heard Union soldiers are up there," Smith said. "We had a fellow living in the apartment up there, and the voices and footsteps shook him up so much that he moved out. He said the racket went on all night."

Union officers from the Twenty-ninth Pennsylvania arrived in Winchester about March 12, 1862, and fought in the First Battle of Kernstown. As

105–107 North Loudoun Street, Miller's Drug Store. *Courtesy of the Handley Regional Library Archives.*

often happened during the War for Southern Independence, officers were quartered in private homes in occupied towns. So it was with the Twenty-ninth, when five men moved into 107 North Loudoun Street.

The voices are purportedly these men arguing over the fate of Joe Boy, a young black man. Our friend, who can communicate with the spirit world, reported that a kangaroo court, consisting of officers from the Twenty-ninth Pennsylvania, is sitting in on the judgment of Joe Boy. The following is her account of the conversation "from beyond." This language isn't mine, and is not intended to offend.

> *"We've got to kill the nigger," one of the Yankees tells his fellow officers.*
> *Another Yankee speaks up, "He has to first confess."*
> *The other responds, "Ok, confess, nigger. You're as guilty as sin. Confess 'cause we're gonna kill you anyway, hang you on that tree out back."*

This is chilling talk for folks seeking freedom for the slaves. My friend picks up on one Yankee's voice that serves as a voice of reason, and she identifies this officer as Boxwell Massey.

"Leave the boy alone. He ain't done nothing, you just want to put the blame on someone."

The other snaps, "Shut your mouth, Massey. We've got to stick together. Joe Boy here is nothing but a nigger, he's guilty as sin and we've got to kill him."

Subsequent research revealed that while the Twenty-ninth Pennsylvania was in Winchester, a young African American was lynched from a tree at 107 North Loudoun Street. Joe Boy was guilty of nothing, yet those soldiers lynched him and watched him struggle for life. They are spirits whose souls will never find peace.

Equally frightening at this site are the sounds created by heavy footsteps. "The sound of those boots always scared me," said a former manager of Stone Soup, who lived upstairs. "For some reason, the boot sounds scared me more than the arguing. Jeannette never scared me, but those heavy boots chilled me to the bone. I could hear them pacing all night. The scariest part was when they came up the steps."

Patrons in V2 have also heard the stomping sounds of boots. "They are followed by a cold, evil chill," said Smith.

Jeanette, Joe Boy and the Yankees are not the only spirits who reside at 107 North Loudoun Street. There is also a writer named Paul Cummings. During the Civil War, Cummings became very ill while living in the attic. He continues to sit at the window watching pigeons.

Also in the attic are two slaves who care for Cummings—Millicent and Victor. Millie seems very jealous of Victor. She wants Mrs. Miller, the owner of the building, to think that she is the one taking care of Mr. Paul.

The former manager of Stone Soup was the first to encounter the attic trio.

The first time I went to the attic was on a very hot day in the summer. I opened the attic door and was hit with a blast of cold air. When I stepped into the room, I saw a man and woman who visibly appeared to be arguing, but I couldn't hear a sound. When I turned to the window, I saw a very sickly man looking out.

I started taking friends to the attic. We were always hit with the icy blast and a few times we would see the three people in the room. The man was always looking out the window while the other two were arguing.

Debbie searched court documents and found that, many years ago, the Miller family did buy a forty-year-old female slave named Millicent.

Giant Indians

Indian Alley, South Piccadilly Street

A LEGEND EXPLAINED

Once upon a time, students in Virginia's public schools learned about a long-vanished race of giant Indians, reported to have been over seven feet tall. The Indians, according to lore, were native to Northern Virginia.

In Winchester, the northernmost city in Virginia, the giant Indians are real, especially to those who have seen them. A walk down Indian Alley, an unobtrusive alley that runs from Cork Street to Piccadilly Street, can be a startling experience. Sightings of very tall Native Americans have been reported there for many years. Testimony indicates that the Indians appear to be very sad and silent.

"They are not from this world," said one Winchester gentleman.

> *I was walking on Piccadilly Street. When I crossed Indian Alley, something caught my eye. I glanced down the alley and out of nowhere I saw a group of very tall Indians walking toward me.*
>
> *They looked like something in a dream. They were a little translucent, but their eyes were what really grabbed my attention. They looked so very sad, as if they had the weight of the world on them.*
>
> *They surely saw me, but they kept walking north. There were five or six of them. I wasn't sure if they were real. I thought maybe they were reenactors. I stepped aside for them to pass, but they were gone, vanished. I just felt cold all over. I've heard legends about giant Indians and every time I walk or drive down Piccadilly Street, I look down the alley, hoping to see them again.*

Sightings of the giant Indians occur in the early evening, late afternoon and early morning hours, while it's still light outside. No one has ever seen them after dark.

This sign is posted on the outside of the George Washington's Office Museum.

The legend began hundreds of years ago. The first written report of such large Indians dates back to 1707, when Swiss explorer Louis Michelle visited the Shenandoah Valley. Local Indians, who lived or hunted in the Winchester area, showed Michelle huge stones, believed to be sacrificial alters. He was also shown burial mounds of ancient warriors known to be over seven feet tall. Though Michelle continued his explorations as far south as Fort Powell, approximately sixty miles from Winchester, giant Indian reports were nonexistent elsewhere. Michelle's diaries and maps relating to his adventures in the Shenandoah Valley are currently stored in the Royal Archives in London.

During the French and Indian War, the tale of the giant Indians was kept very much alive. Colonel George Washington, while in command of the militia force in Winchester, directed the building of Fort Loudoun to protect local citizens from an attack. While digging the fort's foundations, a squad of Washington's militiamen discovered Indian skeletons. Washington reported that the skeletons were seven feet long.

Is the story of the ancient giant Indians a mere legend? Were they among the earliest inhabitants of Winchester? What caused their demise? Most importantly, why do they still roam an unassuming back lane dubbed Indian Alley? This we do know—the giant Indians left an unforgettable mark in Winchester, Virginia.

Lord Fairfax

114 West Boscawen Street
(Christ Episcopal Church Courtyard)

THOMAS, SIXTH LORD OF FAIRFAX

Thomas, the sixth lord of Fairfax, inherited 5,282,000 acres of land in the Northern Neck of Virginia. Born at Leeds Castle in Kent, England, he was the first English nobleman to permanently settle in the new world, about 1735. To control his vast holdings in Virginia, Lord Fairfax built a home, or hunting lodge, in Clarke County, west of the Blue Ridge Mountains. He named his home Greenway Court. Fairfax never married, and folklore has it that he moved to America because he was jilted in a love affair. As a result, he never allowed a woman to enter Greenway Court.

A group of Winchester women hatched a plan to get inside Greenway Court to see how the English nobility lived. The women hired a carriage driver to take them to Greenway Court. As they neared the entrance, the carriage driver stopped and loosened a wheel. In front of the entrance, the wheel conveniently fell off. The ladies thought that surely Lord Fairfax, being of great English nobility, would invite them in while his wheelwright fixed their carriage. Instead, Lord Fairfax sent his staff to set up a tent and serve refreshments to the ladies. The women never entered Greenway Court!

In 1748, Lord Fairfax hired George Washington, a sixteen-year-old surveyor, to help map his land holdings. Popular lore has it that the reason Lord Fairfax hired young Washington was because he liked the way Washington rode a horse.

Although Greenway Court was about fifteen miles from Winchester, the town was the center of Fairfax's business dealings. Winchester was the largest town in the area, and Fairfax spent much of his time in the town. With the advent of the American Revolution, Fairfax, despite his friendship with Washington, remained loyal to the English Crown. Shortly after Washington led the thirteen colonies to their independence,

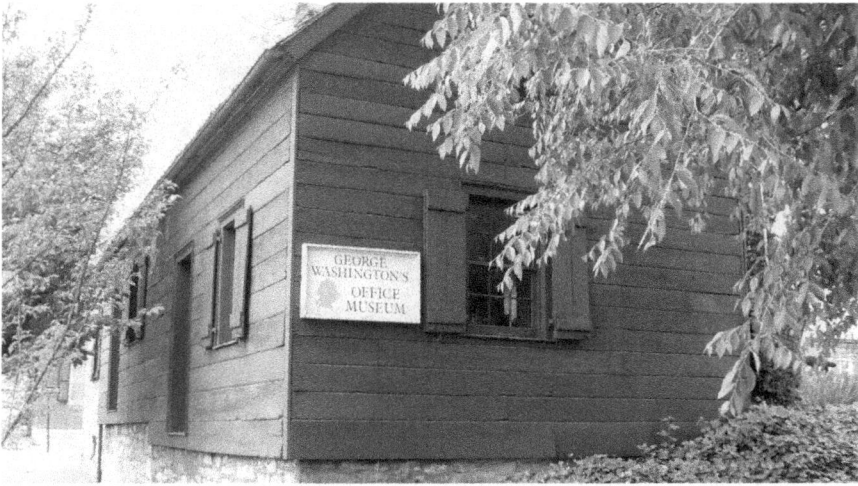

George Washington used this building as his surveying office. He again used it while he directed the building of Fort Loudoun.

Lord Fairfax, while on a business trip to Winchester, became ill and passed away on December 12, 1781.

Fairfax was buried in the Christ Episcopal Church cemetery that, at the time, was located near Loudoun Street in the heart of Winchester. In 1828, the church fathers voted to move the church to its present location at the northeast corner of Washington and Boscawen Streets. Lord Fairfax's body was dug up and taken to the new location, where he was reinterred in the church basement. His remains rested there until 1925. A plan was then devised to honor Fairfax by removing his remains from the basement and placing them in a crypt in a small courtyard on the south side of the church.

How Lord Fairfax came to rest in his new crypt is an unusual story. It was not an easy task to get him from the basement to the crypt. It actually required a little help from the long deceased Thomas, sixth lord of Fairfax himself!

When the plans to move Fairfax were finalized, the church hired a workman to uncover the coffin. Since there was no information as to where the coffin was actually buried, the church took the flooring up, gave the workman a shovel, and said, "Dig until you find the coffin."

After several days, the workman had dug six feet deep in the basement and had found nothing. He finally reported his lack of success to the church fathers, and the shocking reality set in. Perhaps Lord Fairfax had not been removed from his original burial site.

When the chancel of Christ Episcopal Church was enlarged, Lord Fairfax's remains were placed in this new tomb in the church's side yard.

The church paid the workman for his efforts, added extra cash as "hush money," and sent him on his way. It was the end of a most uncomfortable situation. Or was it?

The tired and frustrated workman went home to retire early. During the night, he had a vision. In his dream, the workman received a visit from a very refined gentleman who wore knickers, held a tricorn hat and had silver buckles on his shoes. In a very distinguished voice, the apparition spoke to the workman, "Dig under the partition wall at the far end of the basement and there ye shall find my remains."

After a sleepless night, the workman returned to the church early the next morning. In an animated and shrill voice, he explained that he knew where to find the remains of Lord Fairfax and described what had happened during the night. To humor the workman, the church fathers agreed to let him have one more try. This time, the workman went straight to the spot where the apparition had told him to dig. It was not long before the man uncovered a coffin. The markings on the heavy lead coffin clearly showed it to be the one that held Lord Fairfax's remains. The workman never wavered. He stuck to his story as to how he found the coffin of Lord Fairfax.

So, when you visit Winchester, be sure to see the crypt in the courtyard at Christ Episcopal Church. Remember that it was Lord Fairfax himself who arranged for his own placement in the crypt!

Sword in the Rafter

103 North Braddock Street

O n June 3, 1859, John Brown's arrival in Harper's Ferry set off a chain of events that tormented Dr. Hugh McGuire and his distinguished family in Winchester for decades. Hugh McGuire was the leading doctor of medicine in Winchester. He lived in a stately brick home on the northwest corner of Braddock and Amherst Streets. Two blocks up Amherst Street, Dr. McGuire and his son, Dr. Hunter McGuire, operated the famed Winchester Medical College.

In 1859, our nation was ripped apart by the conflict over tariff issues and antislavery factions. From Kansas came a man who whipped the flames of hate into a roaring fire—John Brown. Brown, a sinister man with a shadowy past, had played a leading role in the troubles of the Bloody Kansas wars. When Kansas became too hot, Brown slipped out of the state and moved to New England. While in New England, he hatched a plot to capture the U.S. arsenal at Harper's Ferry, arm the slaves and lead a revolt to free the slaves in the South. Brown convinced some of the leading abolitionists to back his plan. After collecting the needed money, Brown and a small band of followers, including his sons, Owen, Oliver and Watson, went to Harper's Ferry.

The expected number of supports never arrived, but this did not stop Brown. He and his band actually took the arsenal. However, the taking of the arsenal did little good. The state of Virginia was quick to act by calling out the militia. The U.S. sent Colonel Robert E. Lee to take command of all troops around Harper's Ferry, and the militia company from Winchester was commanded by Lieutenant Colonel Lewis T. Moore, the great-great-grandfather of famous actress Mary Tyler Moore.

On October 18, 1859, Brown and his gang barricaded themselves in the engine house. Jeb Stuart, who had volunteered to serve with Lee in

This was Dr. Hugh McGuire's home. It was here that the good doctor said inkwells floated across the room.

Harper's Ferry, led the assault that killed ten of Brown's followers. The dead included two of Brown's three sons.

After calm returned to Harper's Ferry, students from the Winchester Medical College visited the scene of the action. On a search for cadavers, they claimed the body of one of John Brown's sons and took it to the college in Winchester. Most historians believe the body to have been Oliver. Along with the body, a sword was also claimed. It was taken to the McGuire home, where it was thrust into a rafter in the attic.

Shortly after this episode, strange and mysterious things started to happen to Dr. McGuire. The good doctor recorded the mysterious happenings in his diary. He wrote of furniture being rearranged during the night. He reported that inkwells were lifted off desks and floated across the room. Chairs were pulled out from under people. These bizarre happenings continued throughout the war, as the sword remained thrust in the rafter.

When the war was over, Winchester veterans returned home with plans to end Dr. McGuire's troubles by pulling the sword from the rafter. But, when the brave veterans grabbed the hilt of the sword, they found it icy cold. They were overwhelmed with a fear that, if they pulled the sword from its resting place, something evil would happen to them. Dr. McGuire wrote in his diary that veteran after veteran came to remove the sword, and all had the same experience.

As time rolled by, lads of Winchester went to the McGuire house to have a go at the sword. Each described the icy feeling of the hilt and the fear factor when they attempted to pull on the sword.

During the early 1960s, a young man, who had lived all his life in Winchester and is now a retired vice-president of a local bank, made the attempt.

> *As soon as I grabbed the hilt, I was overcome with fear and cold. It felt like I was holding ice, yet I was sweating so much that it was running down my forehead into my eyes.*
>
> *I was not going to let an old tale beat me. Determined, I gave a mighty tug. It didn't budge, but a feeling of fear came over me. I knew that if I pulled that sword out, something terrible would happen. That sword is best left where it is. There's something evil about it.*

Another witness had this to say,

> *I'd heard about that sword all my life. I remember hearing people talk about how icy it was to touch.*
>
> *It was something I had to find out for myself. I finally got my chance. The second I touched that handle; it was as icy as trying to pick up a block of ice. I knew I didn't want to pull that thing out. It was not a nice feeling. Yes, I gave it a pull, not hard enough to pull the thing out, but I tugged, just to say that I tried. Then I got out of that attic as fast as I could.*

The present owners of the McGuire house just shrug and say nothing is in the attic. This is followed by a sly smile. They admit that they do have the journal kept by Dr. Hugh McGuire.

Prisoners at the Courthouse

20 North Loudoun Street

The old Frederick County Courthouse has a very sad past. Built in 1840, and just twenty-one years old when war descended upon Winchester, its role during the four-year conflict was one of despair. The old courthouse served as both a prison and a hospital, with surgery taking place in the courtroom. It's difficult to imagine all the tortured energy left behind in that courthouse.

After the Third Battle of Winchester, September 19, 1864, the courthouse was captured by Union forces and used as a prison for detained Confederates. At the time, a six-foot-high iron fence encircled the building, and prisoners were confined in the courtyard. The iron fence was removed from the lawn about 1910. During a 1960s restoration of the building, a *Winchester Evening Star* reporter wrote about Union and Confederate soldiers' graffiti on the original plaster walls. Photographed were soldier names, unit numbers and dates.

Today, the Old Frederick County Courthouse houses a privately owned Civil War relic collection. The graffiti, now preserved behind glass, is on view to the paying public. Before the courthouse opened as a museum in 2003, some people walking along the Loudoun Street pedestrian mall claim to have seen a strange and eerie sight. One gentleman, who has witnessed the same sight several times, stated,

> *I walk past the old courthouse many times, but the first time I saw them gave me a scare.*
>
> *I looked at the courthouse as I was passing, and there they were. Pale-like grayish figures were huddled about in the courtyard. Some of them seemed to be holding onto a fence. There also appeared to be guards but, they were more bluish than gray.*

A Ghostly Trip Through the Past

I stopped and rubbed my eyes. When I looked again, they were still there. My next thought was that they must be reenactors. But, they seemed too far away and transparent. A chill ran through me, and I rapidly ran from the scene.

I've seen them several times. I keep walking and try not to look back. Their eyes are very defiant.

Another person who claims to have seen the prisoners said,

Their eyes are depressing and sad. I actually witnessed some of them walking to what appeared to be bars. I watched others stick their hands through the bars.

If you gaze at them long enough, you'll hear terrible cries and screams coming from the courthouse, like someone is being tortured. It's an eerie sound, and makes you feel cold all over.

Inside the courtroom, it is not unusual to hear cries of pain. During the war, painkilling drugs were not always available. Surgery was sometimes performed on men who bit down on a stick. Others were loaded with whiskey. Either way, the pain they endured during amputations must have been relentless, which may explain the cries of torture coming from the building.

During the early days of the courthouse, a hanging tree was located on the north side of the courtyard. Visitors taking the Historic Haunts of Winchester ghost tour are asked to walk down the north side of the courthouse. Nearly every time, one or more in the group describes a coldness that is not natural.

In 2005, Frederick County renovated the courtroom. During restoration, workmen found haversacks, bits of clothing, a Confederate butternut uniform and part of a Yankee frock coat. The workmen also discovered more than artifacts. They frequently heard men arguing and shouting. Additionally, strange things occurred during their lunch breaks. The workers often returned from lunch to find that their tools had been hidden. But the scariest thing was when they returned to find scaffolding had been moved from one side of the room to the other side. Three members of the work force walked off the job.

There are other happenings in the courthouse that have had a frightening effect as well. Sally Coates, the first manager of the museum, became a believer in spirits on the Sunday afternoon that she heard the voices. It was near closing time, and four people, including Sally, were

Built in 1840, the Frederick County Courthouse served as a prison and hospital during the Civil War. Soldiers left graffiti on the walls throughout the building.

in the gift shop. Suddenly, Sally dashed from behind the counter, saying, "Who called me? Who's here?"

She ran into the courtroom, still asking, "Who's calling me?" She then dashed up to the second floor to see if the young lady who was volunteering that day had called her. "No, I didn't call. No, no one has been up here for an hour or so."

Sally returned to the gift shop and asked, "Did anyone hear someone call my name?"

A twelve-year-old boy visitor spoke up, "I did. I heard someone call Sally."

Not long after that, Sally, who sometimes helps with the research for the Historic Haunts of Winchester tour, heard the voice again. This time, I was with her in her office on the second floor of the courthouse. All the doors were closed and locked. Yet, as clear as if someone else was in the office, we heard a voice calling, "Sally, Sally." Sally looked at me and said, "Tell me you heard that?"

A quick search of the building only served to prove that we were the only living people in the courthouse. Nevertheless, the voice we heard was a gentle one. It belonged to a young man.

Another happening in the courthouse is the sound of loud booms. The first time this was heard was on a beautiful, clear Sunday. The sky was crystal blue and cloudless. The first boom was so loud it really garnered attention. After several repeated booms, Sally said, "It sounds like it's going to storm. Listen to that thunder."

To further check out the situation, Sally went outside, where she quickly was convinced that it was not going to rain and what she heard was not thunder. Slowly, she came to the realization—the booming sounds were Civil War cannon!

Since that episode, other visitors in the courthouse have heard the same booming sounds. Why not? After all, Winchester endured bitter war for nearly four years. Likely, the cannon fire is Southern gunners. The sounds seem to come from the South. Four times during the war, Confederates came down the Valley Pike to take control of Winchester from the Yankees.

Are those Southern gunners still trying to drive the Yankees from Winchester?

Pacing Ghost

135 North Braddock Street

During the War for Southern Independence, the Lloyd Logan Home, located on the southwest corner of Braddock and Piccadilly Streets, was the scene of repeated indignities. At the outbreak of hostilities, the Logan House was one of the finest homes in Winchester. When Union commanders controlled the town, they frequently tossed the Logan family out, and moved in. For the Yankees, getting Lloyd Logan out of the way was easy. As a rebel-rousing leader for the Southern cause, Logan was always subject to arrest. He spent much of the war in Union prisons.

In 1862, Union General Franz Sigel had Logan arrested and tossed in jail. He then entered the Logan home, and despite the pleas of Mrs. Logan, he confiscated much of her furniture and used the house for his headquarters.

Later, General Philip Sheridan used the house as his headquarters. But the bleakest days for the Logan family came in the spring of 1863—in the form of Robert Milroy. As local folklore has it, Milroy's wife coveted the Logan Home, and she just had to have it. So, on April 7, 1863, the general ordered the eviction of Mrs. Logan and her daughters. It was a cold, rainy, spring day. A squad of soldiers dressed in blue pulled up in a wagon in front of the Logan home. They ordered Mrs. Logan and her daughters out of the house. At the time, one of the girls was very ill.

The soldiers put the Logan women in the wagon. They were taken to Newtown (known today as Stephens City) and put out in the middle of Valley Pike without a change of clothes or anything to protect them from the rain. Fortunately, the fine people of Newtown quickly took in the women. In the meantime however, Milroy and his wife moved into their home.

Since those troubled times, a strange thing has been recurring in the Logan House. It continues to this very day. When walking or driving along Braddock Street, people glance up at the Logan House and then

The Lloyd Logan House, a famous old Winchester landmark, is located on the west side of Braddock Street.

135 North Braddock. The Lloyd Logan House looked like this before the large front porch and columns were added. *The undated picture is courtesy of the Handley Regional Library Archives.*

focus their eyes on the two windows on the south side of the second floor. What they see in the window is a frightening sight.

"I don't know what made me look at those windows. It seemed that I couldn't do anything but look," said one Winchester man who dared look at the windows. "I looked and there he was, pacing back and forth, throwing his hands over his head. He wasn't really clear, sort of gray and fuzzy. I think he was even pulling at his hair." It's the same story from everyone who has seen the pacing man.

Today, the building houses Kimberly's, an upscale gift shop. Some associates on Kimberly's staff can attest to what's going on in that room on the second floor. While folks on the outside see a man pacing, Kimberly's staff sees the same man pacing on the inside. There is one major difference, however. The staff also sees a very sad looking woman sitting in the corner. She's crying, holding her hands together and watching the man pace.

"The first thing that hits you when you enter that room is the cold," said a member of Kimberly's staff who claims to have seen the two grayish figures.

> *After the cold, you see this guy pacing back and forth. You can almost see through him. While you're watching him pace, you feel, I mean really feel someone else. You look back and, in the corner, you see her. She's just sitting there, crying.*
>
> *They don't seem to notice us or realize we're in the room. I don't think the guy is aware of the woman. But, she is following him with her eyes. For him, something bad has happened.*

Our friend, who can communicate with spirits, visited the room with the pacing man and sensed that "he's very upset. He's pacing because something terrible has happened. A young woman has been killed. I think that's her in the corner. She is related to the pacing man, perhaps a wife or daughter. It was a carriage accident, and it happened at the corner of Amherst and Washington Streets."

A check of old newspapers turned up a carriage accident at that corner in the late 1850s. No name is given, but a woman was killed.

Olde Town Café

Southeast Corner of Loudoun and Boscawen Streets

It Came from the Basement and Out of the Light

Ben, his wife and two daughters moved to Winchester from New York and opened the Olde Town Café in 2005. The brick building, built in 1797 by merchant William Holliday, served as the Winchester Post Office, a dry goods store, a drugstore and several restaurants. One of the restaurants left to relocate two doors south. At one time, the building was also the home of former Governor Frederick Holliday who lost an arm during the Civil War.

Not long after Ben and his family had settled in and started running a smooth operation, the oldest daughter, Beth, headed to the basement for supplies. The door to the basement is cut into the floor, which means one has to reach down and pull the door up. On this particular day, Beth reached down and pulled the door open, only to quickly jump back. Coming up the steps was an unidentified man!

"It scared me," Beth said.

> *He was about halfway up the steps. At first, I couldn't understand how he had gotten there. After all, there is only one entrance to the basement.*
>
> *Just as I started to speak to him, I realized there was something odd about the guy. He was staring straight ahead, like he was looking through me. He was sort of transparent. He was wearing a long coat. I really couldn't tell what time period it was but there was nothing modern about it.*
>
> *As he came up the steps, I took a couple more steps back to let him pass me. He reached the top step and stopped. He kept staring straight ahead, like he was looking for something or someone. Finally, I worked up the nerve and asked, "Can I help you?" He just stopped moving. I think he was aware I was there but he was not concerned about me. I don't know*

This building at 2 South Loudoun Street was constructed in 1797 and is one of the oldest houses in town. At one time, the Winchester Post Office was located here, and in more recent years, it was the site of Boyd's Drug Store.

why I did it but I stepped to the door and closed it. A few minutes later, I re-opened the door but the guy was gone. I went down into the basement but he was nowhere to be found. I called and there was no answer. There is no other way into or out of the basement but through the door in the kitchen.

Since that day, Beth and other members of her family have seen the same man on numerous occasions. He always comes to the top step and stares straight ahead. He never looks from side to side. He never steps across the threshold into the kitchen. He just stands there with a sad expression, then turns and goes back to the basement.

"Through research, we have tried to find out more about him and his connection to the basement. But, nothing comes up in the records," said Beth. "I think he is waiting for something or someone. They or it never come, so he goes back to wait for another day."

The man on the basement steps is not the only strange thing that happens in the Olde Town Café. Old shelves built into the walls in a former era currently serve as bookcases in the restaurant. From time to time, Ben and his family find that their books and other possessions have been rearranged overnight. They also have arrived at work to find the front door open. At first, it was thought the man in the basement was the culprit. "I didn't think so," Beth said. "He wouldn't cross into the kitchen, so why would he do so during the night? The man in the basement, objects mysteriously moving and the door opening by itself were clear signs that we had a ghost or ghosts."

Ben solved the mystery of the door opening and the objects on the shelves being moved late one night when he went to the restaurant to make himself a snack.

It was kind of late, and I was making something, when suddenly there was a very bright light at the door. I thought it was a car, but I soon realized there was no car coming down Boscawen Street.

I couldn't figure it out. As I was watching the light, the front door started to open. It sent cold chills up and down my spine. When the door was fully open, a figure came out of the light. It was a small bent figure wearing a black cloak and hood. The hood was pulled close to the face and I can't be sure but I think it was a woman. She was so small.

She walked over to the shelves and started to rearrange books. She took her time, like she knew where she wanted everything to be.

She never looked my way. She just went about her business. After she finished, she walked across the room into the kitchen but she never looked at me. I'm not sure she was aware I was there. She walked through the kitchen, into the wall, and was gone.

I have no clue as to who she might be. She must have had something to do with the building at one time. She didn't scare me but she did get my attention.

Since that night, Ben has seen the same specter several times. "I don't see her every night that I go to the restaurant. It may be weeks but sooner or later she comes out of the light and does her thing."

The Blue Lady

Melinda, a very charming lady from Leesburg, Virginia, purchased an old building constructed in 1827 in downtown Winchester. She planned to renovate the old house, converting two floors into apartments with a retail store on the first floor. Well into the gutting stage of the process, Melinda encountered disturbing trouble—work was coming to a standstill. Workers refused to go to the loft. It seems that a lady wearing blue was preventing the progression of work. The Blue Lady hid tools, moved equipment and got in the way. Melinda was frustrated.

One of my friends with "the gift" visited and sensed that the Blue Lady used to live with her family in the upper room and she was afraid her living quarters would be destroyed. Melinda was told to explain to the Blue Lady that her living space was going to be improved.

After Melinda properly explained the plans, the Blue Lady actually tried to help with the work. She carried tools to the workers and pointed out things that needed to be fixed. She never spoke. She was described as being an older woman who always wore a bright blue dress. The most unusual attribute was that she was faded. "She looks like an old coat or dress that has started to fade, except you can almost see through her," said one of Melinda's workers. As work progressed, the Blue Lady moved to other rooms where labor was being done. She acted as though she was eager to see the finished project.

Eventually, the apartments were rented and the first floor was turned into an antique shop. The Blue Lady enjoyed being in the antique shop and she enjoyed visiting with one of the upstairs male renters.

The renter, who was the object of this unwanted attention, at first made it a joke. "Tell everyone that my ghostly girlfriend didn't want me to leave tonight. She was reaching out to me, asking me not to go." For a while, her visits were entertaining. But things took a far more serious

This large, prominent building, located at the corner of Loudoun and Cork Streets, proudly proclaims its date of construction. The Blue Lady lives here.

turn. The young gentleman started losing sleep. He became pale and very frightened.

"I can't take this much longer. She's in my apartment all the time. She won't leave me alone. At first, I thought it rather neat to have my own ghost. Well, it's no longer fun. Everything is falling apart. Right now, she's just here, but I have a feeling things could turn bad, especially if I told her to get out."

The young man didn't tell the Blue Lady to leave. Instead, he moved out. And after moving out, his health immediately improved.

Now that the Blue Lady was not tormenting the young man, she caused havoc in the antique shop on the first floor. "She's just here—moving in and out and between things," said the lady who owned the antique shop. "She worries me. I'm not comfortable with her here. She has never caused any problems but I'm sure she can, if she puts her mind to it."

When the ceiling filled up with water and crashed down into the antique shop, no one accused the Blue Lady of doing it. At least not out loud. "It wasn't a lot of damage but it did cause me to wonder."

The antique shop soon moved down the street.

Although nothing has been seen, folks living in the second-story apartments hear strange noises all day and night. "The sounds are like cries of pain and suffering," said one of the second-floor tenants. This is an interesting statement considering the second floor was used as a hospital recovery ward following the Third Battle of Winchester on September 19, 1864.

From the graffiti on the walls, we know members of the Union Nineteenth Corps were housed there. They wrote their names and unit numbers. Sam Marling, a young soldier from the Twenty-second Iowa, wrote that he was a single man looking for a pretty young bride. Marling, wounded at Vicksburg, was transferred to Virginia with his unit and the Nineteenth Corps. They were in town for the Third Battle of Winchester. Marling was a noncombat soldier assigned to the corps hospital. Records suggest that he was perhaps in charge of a hospital ward. The building where Marling scribbled his name on the walls was one block south of the Nineteenth Corps' hospital.

Perhaps the sounds of agony are coming from wounded soldiers recovering from the awful experience of Civil War surgery. Or, maybe there is more.

The current basement was, at one time, above the street. Full-length windows still exist but only a few inches can be seen above the ground. Court documents describe the home as "the three story building facing the Great Wagon Road." The Great Wagon Road was a major road that led settlers from Philadelphia through the Shenandoah Valley to points west.

Additionally, the basement's foundation is made of stone but the 1827 structure is built of brick. It suggests that, at one time, a stone house was on the site.

Going into the basement is a very chilling experience. It is so frightening that Melinda made the decision to leave it alone.

Patsy

38 West Boscawen Street (Formerly G&M Music)

In Winchester the name "Patsy" requires no explanation. It's an affectionate reference to the hometown girl known worldwide as Patsy Cline! With the birth name of Virginia Patterson Hensley, she was born just outside of Winchester, in Gore, on September 8, 1932. She lived at 608 South Kent Street in Winchester.

From Kent Street, the sky was no limit for this local talent star. Patsy started performing in and around Winchester with the Kountry Krackers band. Finally, in the early 1950s, she was a winner on the TV show *Arthur Godfrey's Talent Scouts*. Before Nashville beckoned, Patsy bought her first guitar at the G&M Music store on Boscawen Street. Long before her first smash hit, *Walkin' After Midnight*, Patsy recorded at G&M Music as a teenager.

The day that Patsy was killed in a plane crash in Tennessee on March 5, 1963, was a day the music died. Also killed in the crash were Hawkshaw Hawkins and Cowboy Copas. However, there are those who believe that Patsy is still making beautiful music on the other side.

Her birthday is celebrated annually in Winchester on Labor Day weekend. The event is called Patsy Cline's Birthday Weekend, and the bash attracts hundreds of visitors. A stop at the house in which she lived is a key attraction. Visitors also like to see where she worked and where she performed. The G&M story is a favorite among visitors as well. The building that housed the music store used to be a regular tour stop, but that was before the structure was sold to Grace Lutheran Church.

Thirty years ago, something unusual happened. A group of Patsy fans went to G&M Music and after looking around and asking the usual questions, someone in the group asked if they could see the recording studio. The folks running G&M Music explained that there was nothing in the room as it had long ceased to be a recording studio. The group still insisted that they wanted to have a look around. They were given the okay, and someone took them to the room. Left alone, the tour group closed the door and talked about Pasty as a teenager and her music back in the good old days. After what seemed like an unusually long time, the G&M staff returned to the room. Something was visibly wrong.

"Those people looked scared," said the lady whose family owned G&M. "They looked like the color had been drained from them. They were speechless. We kept asking them what happened in that room. It took a while to get someone to tell us something. Finally, one timid soul spoke up."

We were standing in the middle of the room, when the door opened and closed. It was as though someone had come in, but we couldn't see someone. The next thing was the coldness that we all felt. It was a hot day, and it was warm in the room when we first came in. After the door opened, it was cold.

It got everyone's attention. What happened next was something I'll never forget. I think everyone felt it at the same time. Nearly everybody gasped. We felt the presence of a young Patsy Cline.

She wasn't a thirty-year-old Pasty but a younger Patsy. She was talking to us, telling us about her teen years. She said that no one was ever interested in that part of her life.

From that day on, every day about the time Patsy would have left high school and come to G&M, the back door opened and closed. "She came through the back every day about the same time," said a staff member. "It became a standing joke, 'Here comes Patsy.'" But apart from the door opening and closing, there were no interactions with Patsy.

Until Labor Day. After that first Labor Day happening, someone witnessed a similar teenage Patsy haunting every Labor Day weekend until G&M vacated the building. There were never any other interactions with her—only on the special weekend set aside for Patsy. So G&M staff put it to a test. They frequently asked people to go to the former recording studio throughout the year, but nothing ever happened. But come Labor Day weekend, her presence was felt every time a tour group entered the room that was once a recording studio.

Footsteps

125 West Boscawen Street

This tale comes from the house at 125 West Boscawen Street. It is a story that may convince skeptics that ghosts from the spirit world do indeed walk among us. The house was built before the War for Southern Independence. Town Run, a small creek, flows under the building, and a hidden trapdoor in the first floor leads to the creek, allowing one to slip from the house. Once under the house, one can follow Town Run until it again comes to the surface.

The building was used as a hospital by both Union and Confederate soldiers during the war. Since Winchester changed hands seventy-two times during the war, the trapdoor was likely used as an escape route. "I used to go down through the trapdoor to Town Run, where I have found a lot of Union and Confederate buttons, buckles, and coins," said the former owner of the building. "I found almost everything that a soldier would have carried. I don't think anything under the house has anything to do with what is happening in the house. I just don't feel it."

What happens in the house is very interesting. Almost every morning, people working on the first floor hear strange sounds coming from the bedroom on the west side of the second floor. It sounds like bedsprings creaking. This is followed by footsteps going across the room to the door. The door then opens, and footsteps can be heard walking down the hall. The footsteps then proceed down the stairs. With each step, it feels colder on the first floor. When the footsteps reach the bottom of the stairs, they walk to the front door. There, they pause for several seconds. Then the mysterious steps turn and go back the way they came. As they go up the stairs, the temperature on the first floor slowly rises.

A Ghostly Trip Through the Past

The former owner said,

We never saw anyone; we just heard the steps. It gave everyone cold chills, but we all accepted it, and didn't let it bother us.

I tried to find out what causes the steps. I researched the building, but nothing jumped out. I can't shed any light on who else is occupying this building. I do feel it has something to do with the war. What? I don't know.

The businessman sold the building in 1997 to a lawyer who converted the house into his law office. "There's no such thing as ghosts. Can't be," our lawyer said, when he bought the building. But now he is not so sure about that. It didn't take long for doubt to creep into his thoughts.

We'd been in the building a couple of months when we heard someone walking down the hall. I went to see who was there, and found no one.

The walking didn't stop. Almost every day, we'd hear a cricking noise. Then, footsteps walked across the room, and the door opened. Down the hall, down the steps, the temperature would drop. Then, they'd go back upstairs.

When it first began, I'd go up to see if I could see anyone. I'd see the door open and no one come through the door. I felt a cool breeze pass me.

That's not all that happens to the lawyer and his staff. The coming of new owners also prompted new paranormal happenings. The footsteps continue, but something has now invaded the computer system. One of the legal secretaries said,

The footsteps were bad enough. Now our office stays cold all day, no matter what it's like outside, or how high the heat is. We feel that someone is in the room. We don't see anyone, but we know someone else is with us; it's creepy.

We got used to the footsteps, then the cold, and the feeling that someone else was in the room, but now...this is scary. It all started after we had the feeling that someone else was in the room. We'd be working with the computers, and suddenly, it felt like cold hands grabbed our hands and moved them from the keyboard. Then, the keyboard started working by itself, like invisible hands were typing. We could see the keys moving and, then, the screen would come to life. Words were being

This monument of a Confederate soldier was erected to honor all the Confederate soldiers in Winchester and in Frederick County.

written. The words were words I'd never before seen. Someone was writing something that made no sense to me. It was almost like garble, but it was a language.

That was just the beginning. The computers started to turn on by themselves, the keys would start clicking and something would fly across the monitor. Then, the other computer would answer. It reached a point where we [the two legal secretaries] *could not stay in the office alone. We'd either bring our lunches or go out at the same time.*

At day's end, the secretaries turned off the computer monitors. The next morning when they returned to work, they would find long messages consisting of strange words on the monitors. "It was like they were writing to us, trying to communicate." Many people have seen the writing on the computer screens, but no one seems to know what language it is or from where it comes.

This tale is of ghostly goings-on. But, a more interesting aspect of the story is that the past owner believed in the spirit world, and the present owner rejects the world of ghosts. Yet, they both have the same tale to tell...

Something Lost

116 North Braddock Street
(Formerly Winchester Printers)

In an old building previously occupied by Winchester Printers on the east side of Winchester's famed Braddock Street, a mysterious search occurred daily for many years. When the print shop, located in the back of the building, closed operations for the day, someone or something took possession of the shop.

The president of Winchester Printers stated,

> *After the shop staff left, we'd hear a lot of noise coming from back there. We'd hear boxes being moved and turned over. Everything not bolted down was moved or turned over. It sounded as though someone was looking for something.*
>
> *After the noise stopped, we'd go back into the shop. It felt icy cold. We'd have to restack boxes and put trash back in cans.*
>
> *The entire shop was a mess. It looked as though someone had been going through everything, looking for something. I can't explain it any other way. I never saw anything, but I felt a presence, a very cold presence. At first it was a little scary but after a while, we got used to it.*
>
> *We always put things back in order. It was just something that happened. But, we knew we were not alone in the building.*

When Winchester Printers was preparing to move into its new building, located just out of town, the company president came to his office early in the morning to prepare for the move. Each morning, shortly after he arrived, he heard the front door mysteriously open and close. From his office, he heard footsteps go across the lobby and into the shop.

116 North Braddock. This was the residence of Mrs. Bettie Dandridge, daughter of President Zachary Taylor. *Courtesy of the Handley Regional Library Archives.*

The first time it happened, I jumped out of my chair! I could feel the hair on my head standing up. I couldn't understand how someone got in with the alarm system turned on. I rushed into the lobby, but no one was there. But, it was cold and I could feel a presence. It was the same presence I felt in our shop. If I listened closely, I could hear footsteps in the shop.

It was spooky and more than a little unnerving. I learned to live with it but I started looking forward to the move into our new building.

I didn't miss it at all after we moved. I do wish I knew for sure what it was.

What was happening? Was someone looking for something lost?

In paranormal circles, there is a theory that a ghost or spirit will try to reclaim something that it valued during life. With that in mind, and following a search of old records, we offer an explanation as to what may have been happening in the old Winchester Printers building.

Long ago, Cox's Tavern was in this building on South Loudoun Street. Legend has it that George Washington and General Edward Braddock planned the Fort Duquesne Campaign in this building.

The building that housed Winchester Printers was erected on the site of Bettie Taylor Dandridge's home. Mrs. Dandridge was the daughter of President Zachary Taylor and the sister of Confederate Lieutenant General Richard Taylor. Her home stood back from the road, directly on the site of the print shop.

In 1755, during the French and Indian War—when England fought the French and their allies for control of the American frontier—George Washington was a major in command of the militia forces in and around Winchester. The British had sent Major General Edward Braddock to command the British forces in America. Braddock's plan was to launch an offensive from Winchester to strike at the heart of the French defensive line, Fort Duquesne, near Pittsburgh. Washington, serving as a volunteer aide, helped plan the campaign to attack the French and their allies.

Braddock and Washington led 1,400 British regulars and 449 Virginia militiamen out of Winchester in late June 1755. Braddock, who was used to the stand-up and box formations used in European warfare, was completely unprepared for what he encountered at Fort Duquesne. The French and their allies, using ambush and hit-and-run tactics, were more than a match for the British and American militia. They fired from behind trees, fences, rocks and anything that offered cover.

This type of warfare led to a total British and American defeat on July 9, 1755. The British and Americans left 977 dead and wounded on the battlefield. One of the wounded was General Braddock. Braddock was carried with the retreat, but finally, on July 13, he could go no farther. On his deathbed, Braddock gave Washington his six-foot-long battle sash. He asked Washington to see that the sash always went to a military hero. The general died a short while later. With Washington officiating, Braddock was buried in the middle of the road. Wagons were then driven over the grave to prevent the body from being found by the enemy.

Washington kept his promise. The sash was handed from hero to hero, until it came to Zachary Taylor, major general and hero of the Mexican War. After Taylor was elected president, he gave the sash to his daughter, Bettie Taylor Dandridge. She kept it in her home on Braddock Street.

In the early 1900s, the sash was acquired by Mount Vernon, George Washington's historic home, where it remains to this day.

Recalling the theory that a spirit will attempt to reclaim something it valued in life, we ask: Was the spirit who haunted the Winchester print shop seeking the sash? The sash was lost to someone who valued it, and it was in the Dandridge home at one point.

Who was searching for it? General Braddock? George Washington? Zachary Taylor?

The Stone House

15 North Braddock Street

KELLY'S ANTIQUE SHOP

Not many years ago, Kelly, a beautiful and charming lady with a passion for antiques, opened Stone House Antiques at 15 North Braddock Street. The house dated back to before the American Revolution. Kelly soon learned that antiques were not the only old things in her shop.

"It all started the night before I opened," Kelly said. "I was working late to get ready for the opening, when suddenly a chill came over me and I felt a rush of cold air go past me. It was as if someone had just walked through the room. The hair on my head and the back of my neck stood straight up! I called my husband and asked him to stay on the phone with me until I left the building."

That was only the beginning. A few days later, when Kelly arrived to open the store, she discovered that all the pictures on the wall had been tilted. A ritual began that morning. After that first incident, Kelly had to straighten pictures every morning.

"After a while, I got used to it."

Suddenly, the situation took a very dramatic twist. Kelly had taken a day off, and her mother-in-law, Judy, was running the shop. Judy was with a customer in the back room. The customer looked toward the front room, gasped and asked, "Judy, who's that young girl in the front room? She looks as though she stepped out of 1760."

Judy looked toward the front of the store and saw the girl dressed in Colonial-style clothing. She appeared to be browsing. "I don't know her," Judy replied. "I like her dress. It does look original. Let's go see who she is."

Though they never let the young girl out of their sight, she was not to be found when Judy and the customer entered the front room. "The girl in the Colonial-style dress was gone! We both saw her. She couldn't have gone out without us seeing her leave. But, in the brief seconds that it took us to walk to the front room, she disappeared," explained Judy.

After that, the girl was seen several more times. She always appeared in the front room or on the stairs. Some time later, Kelly's landlady stopped by to see how things were going. Kelly told her business was better than expected. The landlady asked Kelly if anything unusual ever happened. Kelly explained her morning ritual with the pictures. With a mischievous look, the landlady asked if anyone had ever seen a young girl in a Colonial dress. When Kelly told her about the several sightings, the landlady laughed and said, "That's my ghost. She has been around this house for a long time, and she had something to do with the Hessian prisoners."

Kelly's landlady explained that during the American Revolution, Hessian prisoners had done the stonework at the house, covering the log house with stone. At that time, Winchester was a holding area for captured Hessians—German soldiers who were paid to fight for the British. She further explained that many of the downtown stone buildings were the work of the Hessian prisoners.

Later, in a deep windowsill facing Braddock Street, Kelly placed some very old and fragile glassware. The next morning, Kelly's heart broke when she found the glassware shattered to pieces. While looking at the shattered glass with a friend, a cold presence passed between them. Kelly looked at her friend and asked, "Did you feel that?" Her friend indicated that yes, she felt it too. Kelly closed the store and left for the day.

Destruction of her fine antiques was the last straw for Kelly. A short time after that incident, Kelly moved her store out of the stone house. "I could handle living with a ghost, but when it started destroying things, I was out of there," Kelly said.

But, wait…this is not the end of the tale.

After Kelly's departure, a jewelry store moved in. The store was open by appointment only. The people who ran the store would not talk about ghosts, nor would they talk to anyone interested in the paranormal. But three years later, a Winchester lawyer bought the building and set about restoring it. The lawyer said,

> *I can tell you why the former owners wouldn't talk with anyone. They didn't want anyone to know what happened here. They thought it would hurt business. But, they saw the girl several times a day.*
>
> *They were willing to live with that. But, when the ghost started breaking things, they moved out.*

Presently, work on restoring the building is going at a snail's pace. "It's difficult to work in there," said one of the guys involved in the restoration project.

> It's downright creepy. We can be doing some very tricky work that requires a lot of concentration, when we suddenly feel a presence. It gets cold, and often, I feel as if someone is looking over my shoulder.
>
> Then, there is the noise. Too often, we hear footsteps going up and down the stairs, doors opening and closing, and things being rattled around. We take a lot of breaks.
>
> It's clear to me that someone—someone we can't see—is in there with us.

The Angel Tillie

33 North Loudoun Street

In Winchester, it's not unusual to see people dressed as though they belong to a past era. You might observe someone who looks like he stepped out of 1764, or you might see someone from 1940. But, what you most likely spot are Civil War reenactors carrying muskets and wearing gray and butternut uniforms about downtown. It's a good plan on the part of Winchester to have characters from its past still walking the streets. But, are they all *really* reenactors?

If you happen to be in front of 33 South Loudoun Street, and you suddenly witness a young girl dashing from the building, wrapping a shawl about her shoulders as she hurries north along Loudoun Street, you have just seen Tillie Russell. Tillie is again rushing to the Rutherford's Farm battle site—just as she did on July 20, 1864. It's a four-mile trek for which Tillie will be known forever as the "Angel of the Battlefield."

Rutherford's Farm, on July 20, 1864, was the place where, in a surprise assault, Union Major General William W. Averill's infantry and cavalry forces attacked Major General Stephen D. Ramseur's division. It was a Union victory that sent Ramseur through Winchester in a confused state.

Fiercely wounded in the assault, Captain Randolph Ridgeley, of the Second Virginia Volunteer Infantry, was not expected to survive the coming night. Tillie found the injured captain and nursed him through the night. When morning came, Tillie was seen holding Ridgeley's head in her lap. Ridgeley was alive and would remain so because of "the Angel."

Tillie's dedication on the battlefield is historically factual. What is far less clear is how Tillie came to be on the field. There are two accounts that trace Tillie from Winchester to Rutherford's Farm. The first comes from Tillie's sister, Lucy Russell. Lucy records that a Confederate surgeon, A.E. Love, asked the ladies of Winchester to volunteer to go to the battle site

Tillie Russell, "Angel of the Battlefield," lived in this building located at 33 South Loudoun Street.

and nurse the wounded. Lucy says that Tillie was one of the volunteers. The second account is far more romantic. This tale comes from Major Henry Kyd Douglas, who wrote about Tillie in his well-known book, *I Rode With Stonewall.*

Douglas wrote that after the battle, when the Confederates were in retreat, he was reluctant to leave Ridgeley alone, fearing he would die. Douglas rode hard to get to Winchester. While going down Loudoun Street, the only person he saw was Tillie. Douglas says he pulled up in front of the Russell home to talk with Tillie. "Tillie," Douglas cried out, "Will you go out to Rutherford's Farm, find Captain Ridgeley, and see to it that he gets to a hospital?" Douglas watched Tillie for a moment, and then realized she was going alone. "I never dreamed she would go alone," Douglas said.

With that, Douglas spurred his horse and was off. Tillie quickly turned back into her house, picked up a shawl and, wrapping the shawl about her shoulders, returned to the street. Did Tillie know Captain Ridgeley? Or was it a true Southern woman's heart that drove her to the battlefield that day?

As the years continue to pass by, more and more people witness the young woman emerging from the building at 33 South Loudoun Street. She steps into the street and scurries north. People state that there is a look of urgency in her eyes. Some people claim to have watched her until she is no longer in sight.

Robin, who ran a doll store at 33 South Loudoun Street, says that she often looked up to catch a glimpse of a young woman stepping through the door while wrapping something about herself. Sometimes, Robin approached visitors passing by and asked if they saw a young woman in Civil War–period clothes. Almost every time, someone claimed to have seen the woman hurrying down the street. Robin said,

The first time I saw her, I thought she was a reenactor and something was going on downtown. It happened so suddenly. I looked up to see a young woman in period dress. It was late in the afternoon when I saw her. Just before going through the door, she glanced back.

Her eyes, I'll always remember those eyes. I've never seen such determination. She's clearly a woman on a mission. More than anything, I can't forget her eyes. When I saw them, I knew I was looking into eyes not of this world. She was a very pretty girl. I've seen her a lot since then, and you know she's only passing through. I think sometimes she even smiles at me.

A Night on the Battlefield. Tillie over a wounded solider. *A drawing by M.K. Kellogg, courtesy of the Handley Regional Library Archives.*

So, which of the two stories rings true as to how Tillie came to be at Rutherford's Farm? Perhaps Tillie is trying to answer that for us, from the grave.

There are two wonderful drawings of Tillie holding Captain Ridgeley: One is by Oregon Wilson (entitled *Woman's Devotion*) and the other by M.K. Kellogg (entitled *A Night on the Battlefield*).

In Winchester, Tillie will always be the "Angel of the Battlefield."

The Arlington Hotel

151 North Loudoun Street

A PENNY

It all started the day Kris opened Confetti, her party supply store, situated at 151 North Loudoun Street. At the appointed hour of 10:00 a.m., Kris opened for business. She was behind the counter, excitedly awaiting her first customer, when suddenly the front door was loudly pushed open, and footsteps raced into the store and dashed upstairs. Then, all the water in the bathroom was turned on.

> *When I heard the door open, I looked up. No one was there, but I heard what sounded like someone running into the room and up the stairs. It became very cold in the room, like a presence of some kind had come in.*
>
> *My heart was pounding like crazy. When I heard the water running in the upstairs bathroom, I got out of there. I went outside to wait for my business partner—my mother.*

Kris's mother arrived and found her daughter standing outside on the street. Of course, the first question was, "Why?" Kris explained what had happened. Her mother told Kris that it was nothing—just a mind trick. She promised to open the store the next day.

The following day, as Kris arrived at the store, she found her mother standing outside on the street. "She was scared and shaking like a leaf," Kris said.

> *She had experienced the same thing! It happened every day, right after we opened up. It was scary. The door was pushed open so violently that we didn't know what to expect.*
>
> *We decided to stick it out, hoping it would just stop. I thought it was a spirit telling us he didn't want us here. I wasn't going to let a ghost chase us out.*

The building had at one time, before the War for Southern Independence, been the Arlington Hotel. "I did some research, trying to find an explanation, but I found nothing. It was scary; we never felt comfortable," Kris said.

As time passed, the unseen visitor continued to make his early morning presence felt. Nothing else happened other than the door opening, the footsteps racing across the room and upstairs and the running water. As a result, the women's fear gradually slipped away and all was fine… until several months later. Kris and her mother had hired a lady to help with the store. With the coming of another person in the store, the situation took a turn for the worse. From her first day of employment, the newcomer felt someone pinching her on the arms. To offer proof, she revealed that her arms were black and blue from the wrist to the elbow.

"She didn't stay with us long," Kris said. "We hired someone else, and she was pinched as well."

To commemorate their first Halloween in the party supply store, Kris and her mother agreed to open Confetti at night for a Halloween ghost tour. When the tour group arrived, Kris and her mother were down on their knees, picking up merchandise. The two women had frightened looks on their faces.

Finally, Kris looked up and said, "We went out for dinner, and when we got back, everything that had been on the shelves was on the floor. The doors were locked; the alarm was turned on. Still, someone came in and cleared off the shelves."

Not only was everything off the shelves, but also the very large plastic Frankenstein that guarded the front door and the huge Godzilla that guarded the back door were in the middle of the room. They were clutching at each other as through they were fighting!

"That's scarier than all the stuff on the floor," Kris said. "Someone moved them while we were out. But who, or better yet, *how* did they get into the middle of the store together?" The situation was indeed baffling.

Two years went by and the front door continued to open, footsteps continued to dash up the stairs and the water in the bathroom still ran at full force. But Kris and her mother felt they were settled in with their ghost. Then, a penny was found!

One morning, following the usual ghostly visit, Kris went upstairs and found a penny in front of the bathroom door. Thinking nothing of it, she picked up the penny and continued on with her work. The next day, right on schedule, the unseen visitor did his thing and again left a penny. From then on, a penny was found following each morning visit.

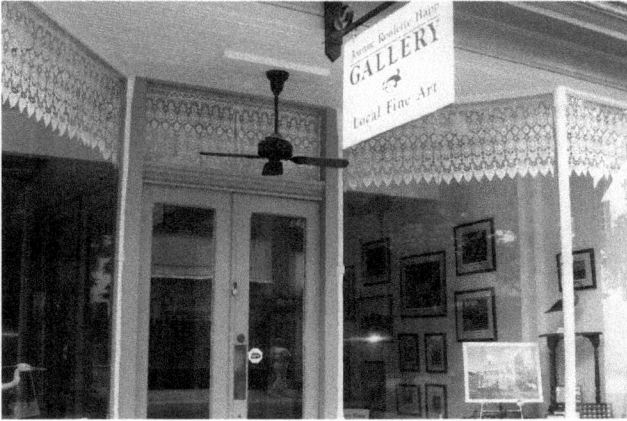

This vintage fan, suspended just outside Joanne Happ's Gallery, is the last remaining fan of its kind on the Loudoun Street mall. Joanne says it was probably used to keep flies out of Anderson's Meat Market, located just south of the Arlington Hotel.

"We thought it was strange, but I wasn't going to tell a ghost to stop leaving pennies," Kris said.

The routine continued every day, like clockwork, for the next year. Then, a new twist was added to the scenario. As a party store, the sale of costumes was an important part of Confetti's business. Mannequins—male and female—were used to creatively display the costumes. When they weren't "dressed," the mannequins were stored on the second floor, near the bathroom. One day, when the ghostly visitor made his daily dash, he left a penny in front of the bathroom, as usual, and also left one on each breast of the female mannequin. "That was the last straw," explained Kris.

Was this a male spirit with a sense of humor?

It didn't take long for Confetti to relocate across the street. "Since we moved, we haven't had any trouble," said a smiling Kris.

But there is more.

After Confetti moved, two gentlemen who hailed from New Orleans took an option on the building at 151 North Loudoun Street. They planned to open a restaurant that featured a Cajun-style menu. Equipment was moved in, and a big story featuring the restaurant was published in the *Winchester Star*. Suddenly, the project was disbanded! The two men from New Orleans quickly left town. The only thing we know about the situation came from a very brief statement. The gentlemen said, "This is not the location we had hoped it would be."

Retreating Yankees

Joseph Denney Residence (Currently an empty lot between 21 and 31 South Braddock Street)

YANKEES ON THE RUN

During the early morning hours of May 25, 1862, Major General Thomas Jonathan "Stonewall" Jackson hurled his exhausted Valley Army against the Union forces commanded by Major General Nathaniel Banks one last time. The assault was spearheaded by a flanking move by the Louisiana Brigade under the command of Brigadier General Richard Taylor. Taylor's brigade turned the right flank of the Union forces on Bowers Hill, causing the Yankees to abandon their position. This led to a full-scale retreat.

As the whole of Jackson's Valley Army surged forward, the Yankee retreat turned into a riot. The Federal forces hotfooted it through Winchester, running down Braddock and Loudoun Streets. As the battered Yankees were streaming down Loudoun Street, General Banks rushed out of the Taylor Hotel and attempted to rally his forces. "My God, men, my God, don't you love your country? Stand and fight!" Banks shouted.

One retreating soldier turned to Banks and said, "Yes, General, we love our country and we're trying to get back to it as fast as we can."

Not all of the Union men were trying to get back across the Potomac as quickly as they could. Many a Yankee soldier was holding ranks and willing to turn and fight. Yet no officer seemed to be willing to lead them.

It appears that the Yankees who were willing to stand and fight are still with us. During the dead of night when all is quiet, those few people who are up at such hours have encountered a strange and eerie sight on Braddock Street. In the two blocks between Cork and Boscawen Streets, people see a large body of Union soldiers hurrying north along Braddock Street. They are holding formation; their muskets are at the ready.

Most people think they are seeing reenactors. But a closer look reveals eyes of defiance and terror. One leading citizen of Winchester stated,

The first time I saw them, I thought I was sleepwalking or dreaming. I couldn't sleep, so I took a walk. Just as I turned from Boscawen onto Braddock Street (going south) I saw a large body of men. They scared me. I couldn't figure why so many men were coming toward me at that hour.

I stopped to see what they were doing. They kept coming toward me. I rubbed my eyes, but they were still there. As they got closer, I could see they appeared to be wearing some kind of blue uniform and carrying guns.

I backed up against the wall of Rouss Fire Hall and waited. The closer they came, the more I thought they were reenactors. But, when they came up to me, I could see their faces. They looked very hard and defiant. Their eyes were what made me think twice about them being reenactors. Their eyes were terrible, filled with fear.

They were moving fast, but they were in formation. They had what appeared to be muskets at some sort of ready position. I do believe that if anyone tried to stop them, they would have put up a fight. They looked like a bunch of rough and tough customers.

I couldn't put them out of my mind. A few nights later, I was up late, so I decided to see if they were still there. It was about four o'clock and, sure enough, here they came again. I was more alert this time and I saw the same thing, the same faces. I did notice that it was very cold while I watched them. It was a warm night, but I was cold. After they passed by, it seemed warm again.

They never looked at me. They just stared straight ahead. I don't know who or what they are, but it's spooky.

Since then, I have talked with others who go for late-night or early-morning walks. They all have seen the same thing! Their descriptions match mine to a T.

There are no reports of anyone seeing these apparitions during the daylight. It's only late at night or early in the morning, before dawn, while darkness still grips Winchester. An interesting aspect of the sightings is that most of them occur near the site of Joseph Denney's home. Denney was a Union sympathizer who lived along Braddock Street during the Civil War. When the Yankees controlled Winchester, the Northern newspapermen who followed the armies often stayed at the Denney home. Perhaps those Yankee newspapermen are still watching their soldiers retreat.

Historically, the only time Union forces retreated along Braddock Street was during the First Battle of Winchester. It was the major victory of Jackson's legendary Valley Campaign, which pulled troops away from

Union and Confederate soldiers alike frequented the Palace Bar, one of Winchester's finest ordinaries. The Palace Bar is now a part of the Feltner Community Foundation at 9 Court Square.

the Yankee advance on Richmond and gave the Confederacy breathing room. It also gave Robert E. Lee time to prepare for his campaign (now known as the Seven Days Battle).

It is a known fact that when the Yankees retreated along Braddock Street they held their formations. Not until they reached a couple of blocks from the center of town did they break and run. Once they started running, they did not stop until they reached the Potomac. Oh yes, General Banks was one of the first Yankees to reach the Potomac.

Jackson led the pursuit as far as Stephenson's Depot.

"I can't say I was afraid of them, but they did scare the hell out of me," said another witness of the Yankees on the run. "I know now that I saw ghosts. Still, it was thrilling to see them. It was like watching history march past. I just wish I could see some Confederate spirits or ghosts. That would really be something!"

Ghosts of Braddock Street Church Parking Lot

Southeast Corner of Braddock Street at Wolfe Street

PHANTOMS IN THE PARKING LOT

During the French and Indian War, Winchester was the frontier command post for the defense of Virginia, and George Washington was in command of the local militia charged with defending Winchester from a possible attack. Washington built two forts—Fort Loudoun, his main defensive fort, and Fort George, his main in-town fort.

Today, the Braddock Street Methodist Church, located on the southwest corner of Braddock and Wolfe Streets, stands on the site of Fort George. Washington also constructed smaller stone forts throughout the Winchester area. Many of these small stone forts still stand today—but forts do not play a role in this tale.

Across the road from the Braddock Street Methodist Church is the church's parking lot. Before the church acquired the land for its parking lot, the site was the home of the Grand Piano Furniture store, destroyed by fire about a decade ago. Almost 250 years before, Washington used the land as a training ground to whip his raw militia recruits into military shape. Most Winchester residents do not know that he once used the lot for military tactics. That fact will play a major role in our tale.

Several years ago, a young woman opened a psychic shop located on the southeast corner of Braddock and Wolfe Streets—across from the church parking lot. To promote her paranormal shop, the lady organized psychic retreats. The first retreat was made up of people from Baltimore who had the "psychic gift." Two weeks later, a group from Washington, D.C., was scheduled to participate in a retreat.

During the first Saturday afternoon retreat, something caught the eye of one of the psychics from Baltimore. He went outside to check out the parking lot and was soon joined by the other psychics. They spent the rest of the daylight hours watching what appeared to be Colonial soldiers rehearsing military drills in the empty parking lot. A few telephone calls turned up an explanation. Yes, George Washington had used that area as a drill field for his raw recruits.

"That explains what we've been watching," said one of the psychics.

Two weeks later, the group from Washington, D.C., also saw the Colonial phantoms. Since then, investigation has revealed several other sightings of Colonial soldiers. Employees and customers of the old furniture store reluctantly admitted to seeing rugged-looking men dressed for war wandering about the store. One former employee stated,

It was the strangest thing. They would just be there. They looked confused and unsure of themselves.

I don't know about drill, but they did appear to be trying to do something. They'd shift their guns, walk or try to march.

It seemed the furniture was in their way and they didn't know what to do about it.

The employees got used to it after a while. It did scare some of our customers. They'd be looking at furniture, when suddenly a strange looking guy dressed in Colonial clothes would march past. Oh yes, it turned cold in the building when we saw them.

For a long time, I thought it was the way the light came in the windows, late in the afternoon. You know how light can play tricks on you? I didn't believe in ghosts at the time, but it did scare the customers.

This employee, in time, came to change his mind about ghosts.

When people came in and asked about our ghosts, I'd smile and talk about ghosts. I let them believe we had Colonial ghosts.

That all changed on one slow day. I had nothing to do but walk around and straighten the furniture. All of a sudden, I felt, what seemed like, very cold, rough and strong hands grab me by the shoulders and shove me aside. When I looked around, I saw what appeared to be three Colonial soldiers marching past me. I'll never forget how those hands felt.

It took me by total surprise. I knew they were not tricks of the light. It did scare me. I asked around among the other salesmen. Several admitted having the same kind of experience. None of them really wanted to talk about it. No one really wants to admit to a ghostly experience.

From then on, I stayed out of the middle of the paths between the furniture, especially when I saw the images that I thought were

George Washington's picture hangs on a wall in the Winchester Hiram Lodge No. 21. Chartered in 1768, it is the oldest Masonic lodge west of the Blue Ridge Mountains.

caused by the late afternoon light. I got out of their way and let them do their thing.

I can now admit that I saw ghosts. After I accepted the fact that they were ghosts, I watched them a lot closer. They seemed very confused around the furniture and often they'd walk right through it. Other times, they moved it aside and out of the way.

It was interesting to watch customers when they had experiences, too. At times, they stumbled and acted as though they were shoved. They'd look to see who shoved them, then gasp. They usually left the store very quickly.

The one question no one asks about the drilling soldiers is this: Who is in command, and is he riding a white horse?

George Washington, of course, always rode a white horse. A Winchester historian, now deceased, always became frustrated upon hearing that someone failed to ask about the white horse. He often mused, "Wouldn't it be something if we could prove George Washington's ghost was in Winchester?"

Perhaps, some day, someone will do just that!

The Galloping Ghost

Outside the City of Winchester

10:00 P.M.

During the latter part of the nineteenth century, Godfrey Lewis Miller was one of the leading doctors in Winchester and the surrounding area. One night, Dr. Miller received an urgent message from a family in Frederick County. The family's teenage daughter was dying.

A message was sent back to the family informing them that the good doctor was on his way. Dr. Miller harnessed his buggy and slowly made his way out of town. It was quiet and still, a perfect night to be out. Halfway to his destination, Dr. Miller was suddenly startled. A horse was galloping toward him. He pulled aside to wait and see if the rider was bringing news from the family about his patient.

Out of the darkness came a girl, riding bareback and heading toward Winchester. The doctor wondered why a family would allow the young girl to ride bareback into Winchester at such a late hour. What time was it? Dr Miller pulled out his watch and saw that it was 10:00 p.m. Then, he suddenly realized that the girl on the horse was the young lady whom he was to visit. Dr Miller became very angry. He called out to the girl, but she continued past him, without an acknowledgement.

Instead of turning back to town, the good doctor decided to have a few words with the family. He picked up the pace and soon he was pounding on the farmhouse door. When the girl's father opened the door, Dr. Miller launched a verbal attack.

According to the written record, this is what transpired:

> *"How dare you call me out this time of night and for no reason,"*
> *shouted the doctor. "Right now, there may be someone who is in need*
> *of my services, yet here I am for no reason. Why did you send for me?"*
> *The doctor was indignant.*

The father was stunned. "Doctor, what are you talking about? I assure you that our call was one of serious need."

The doctor interrupted, "Just minutes ago, I passed your daughter riding toward town. Why did you allow her to do such a thing?"

The father was taken back. "What do you mean, Sir? Our daughter is in the parlor. She passed away at 10 o'clock sharp!"

Doctor Miller was speechless. He told the grieving family what happened on the way from town. He humbly apologized and asked to see the dead girl. When shown the girl, a cold chill ran through the doctor. The dead girl not only looked like the girl he had seen riding toward town, but she was wearing the same dress!

For the rest of his life, Dr. Miller was haunted by this bizarre incident.

Cards by Candlelight

28 South Loudoun Street, Godfrey Miller Home

Godfrey Sperry Miller was a man of strange ways. His behavior often landed him in trouble with his family and much of Winchester. Behind closed doors, there was talk that Miller was perhaps involved in things that were best left alone. Miller and his family lived in a magnificent stone house at 28 South Loudoun Street. Built sometime between 1785 and 1800, the home was conveyed to Godfrey in 1857, following the death of his father.

In 1934, Godfrey's unmarried daughter, Margaretta, became the sole owner of the property. Upon her death in 1938, Margaretta willed the house to the Lutheran Church to be used as an "old ladies' home." For twenty years, the wishes of Margaretta's will were carried out, and during that time nearly fifty ladies enjoyed living in one of Winchester's grand old homes. Or rather, they *should* have enjoyed living in such a magnificent home.

A very strange thing took place in the house. Every night, the ladies were apparently aroused from their slumber by sounds of footsteps coming up the stairs and then progressing down the hall to an unused room in the front of the building. Then, the door allegedly opened and closed and voices were heard. The voices came from men who were talking and laughing.

No one ever understood why the room was not used by the ladies. Since the death of Godfrey Miller, it had not been used. Legend has it that Godfrey Miller used the room for his poker games. Late at night, he habitually brought his peculiar friends home to play poker. They were loud and, at times, rowdy.

It was whispered that Miller and his friends still used the room to play poker.

It is said that Godfrey Miller and his friends still play cards in an upstairs room of this stately building located at 28 South Loudoun Street.

As time passed, the footsteps and loud talking became too much for the elderly ladies. They decided to take a peek into the room. Late one night, after the footsteps of several people had made their way to the room, the ladies followed. They saw a dim light shining under the door. One bold lady reached out and turned the door handle. A gasp followed. What the ladies saw was a group of men sitting around a table playing cards by candlelight. The men looked up, smiled and some even waved. Then, they went back to playing cards.

This scene repeated itself every night for years. It finally reached the point where the ladies became uncomfortable living in a house that they shared with ghosts. The home now functions as an adult fellowship center. Future plans include the development of a museum, too.

No one knows for sure who those men were, but the late Judge Robert Woltz had his opinion. "No doubt, it is Miller and his cronies," said Woltz. "He was known to play cards late at night. Plots like his are best left in the past."

Red Lion Tavern

204 and 208 South Loudoun Street

DANKE

Famous people who helped to shape our country frequently stopped at the Red Lion Tavern for food, drink and conversation. Located at 204 South Loudoun Street, the tavern was opened about 1783 by Peter Lauck, owner and operator. He and his brothers, Simon and Abraham, were natives of Germany and came to Winchester prior to the American Revolution.

During the Revolutionary War, the Lauck brothers were members of Daniel Morgan's Riflemen. It was the Riflemen who helped Morgan win the Battle of Cowpens, opening the way for the British surrender at Yorktown. After independence was won, Peter Lauck and other German members of the Riflemen, affectionately referred to as the "Dutch Mess," held reunions to commemorate the siege of Quebec. They got together yearly on Lauck's birthday for an evening of food, drink and old war stories. The reunions were always held at the Red Lion Tavern.

The Red Lion Tavern is now an office building, but spirits from the bygone era are still lurking. Not so long ago, in the offices on the south side of the building, a gentleman was working late. Finally, with weary and aching eyes, he decided that he had done enough work for one night. He went down the stairs, stopped and turned out the lights at the bottom of the stairs. From the landing, he heard a soft, young female voice say, *"Danke."* The man thought nothing of it. After all, he was extremely tired.

The next time that he worked late, he heard the same voice say, *"Danke."* The man said,

> *The second time, she got my attention. After the third time, I told a co-worker, who often worked late, about my experience.*
>
> *She told me that she had also heard a young female voice say something in German. She said that, when she first heard the voice, she couldn't move. Finally, she turned the lights back on, but she saw no one.*

This memorial and gravesite of General Daniel Morgan is one of the most visited graves in Mount Hebron Cemetery.

Many years ago, famous people dined at the Red Lion Tavern.

She was afraid people would make fun of her, if she mentioned anything about it.

I thought it might be Molly, another co-worker, playing games. I came up with a plan to catch her. I turned out the lights and, as soon as I heard the voice, I turned the lights on again. Nothing—no one could have disappeared so fast. I had the lights back on in a split second, yet no one was there. Another thing, it always seemed very cold after the voice spoke.

The voice continued, but no one was really afraid. It was something that just happened on that landing. The problem was that no one understood German. Therefore, they did not know the meaning of *danke.* Tara, a young German student, provided the answer. "*Danke* is one of three ways to say thank you in German," Tara explained.

After that, the shadowy shape of a young woman or girl was seen whenever *danke* was heard. "She is only there for a second," said an employee who has seen her more than once. "But, she looks to be in a Colonial-style dress."

Does that explain the mysterious voice? We know that Peter Lauck had seven daughters. Could one still be lingering behind for reasons that only she knows?

The Redheaded Woman Still Waits

When our nation was young, everyone passing through Winchester stayed at the Taylor Hotel. In its day, it was the rival of any prestigious hotel in our country. Famous people such as Henry Clay, Daniel Webster and Chief Justice John Marshall stayed at the Taylor. Clay and Webster delivered speeches for Winchester citizens from the balcony of the Taylor, while Marshall took a stick to a young lawyer in the lobby.

Popular folklore has it that Abraham Lincoln stayed at the Taylor on his way to Washington, following his election to Congress in 1848.

During the War for Southern Independence, generals from both North and South used the Taylor. In May of 1862, Union Major General Nathaniel Banks stayed at the Taylor while his troops were being battered on Bowers Hill, just south of Winchester, during the First Battle of Winchester.

Confederate General Thomas J. "Stonewall" Jackson stayed in suite 23 of the Taylor at least three times. Suite 23 consisted of four rooms, two on the second floor and two upstairs. The suite is still there, but it was abandoned long ago.

Jackson's first stay was during the winter of 1861, when his small army was stationed in Winchester. It was at the Taylor Hotel, a stagecoach stop, that Jackson greeted his wife, Mary Ann, when she came to spend the winter with her general. The couple did not stay at the hotel. Instead, Jackson arranged for rooms with the Reverend James Graham and his family.

Jackson's second stay followed the First Battle of Winchester. After an all-night running fight with the Union forces, who were retreating from Strasburg, and the battle the next day, Jackson pursued the retreating Yankees as far as Stephenson's Depot. Upon his return to Winchester,

This scene, which includes a horse and buggy in front of the Taylor Hotel, was likely a familiar sight in downtown Winchester for many years. *The undated picture is courtesy of the Handley Regional Library Archives.*

Jackson went straight to suite 23, fell on the bed in full uniform and boots and slept for twelve hours.

His final stay came later in 1862, during the fall following the Battle of Sharpsburg.

Today, the old hotel stands empty. No great men walk its halls or enjoy its food and drink. It is a decaying reminder of times past, when it was one of the finest hotels in the nation. A search of the building for mementos of the past turned up a very broad bow tie with orange roses and parts of newspapers with an 1859 date. Thus far, nothing has been found to link Jackson to suite 23, but no thorough search has been made.

As desolate as the building looks from the outside, it is far from empty on the inside. People who lived before the war and during the war still walk the halls or patiently wait. Our lady friend with "the gift" found that a prostitute still roams the floors looking for work. Also, some employees from the last company that occupied the building have reported strange happenings.

One former Intelos employee gave this account:

Turner Ashby. *Courtesy of the Handley Regional Library Archives.*

There were noises, strange noises like voices and dishes rattling. You could almost feel other beings. They didn't seem to care about us; they were doing their thing. I always hoped to see something, but I never did. I could feel them, but not see them. A couple of my co-workers had experiences they would not discuss.

Yet, the strangest of all things in the Taylor Hotel, as reported by "the gifted one," is the redheaded woman who is in suite 23 waiting for the general to return.

For which general does she wait? Banks? Jackson? Perhaps Turner Ashby?

It was in the Taylor Hotel that Ashby, commander of Jackson's cavalry, received his commission as a brigadier general from Sandy Pendleton. Jackson refused to hand the commission to Ashby because he believed Ashby lacked discipline.

Walking past what was once the Taylor Hotel can cause chills on the back of the neck. If one goes inside the building, one can feel the presence of long departed souls.

The Sword of Frank Jones

When war came, young men in the South couldn't wait to enlist to fight the Yankees. After all, a Rebel could lick ten Yankees, and the war would be over in three months. The men of Winchester were no different. Everyone was in a rush to join the army before it was too late. One such young man was Frank Jones, a well-connected leader of men. Jones enlisted with the Second Virginia Volunteer Infantry. The Second was one of five regiments of the Stonewall Brigade. Jones was quickly promoted to major and marched to war under the command of Stonewall Jackson. After serving with the Second at First Manassas, then in the Shenandoah Valley, Jones was still with the Second when Jackson's Valley Army was called to Richmond.

As soon as Jackson's forces reached the Richmond area, Robert E. Lee, commander of all the Confederate troops in Virginia, hurled Jackson's men against the right flank of the Union Army of the Potomac, beginning the Seven Days Battle.

The war came to an end for Frank Jones during the fighting around Richmond. His body was returned to Winchester, and he is buried, along with three thousand Confederate soldiers, in the Stonewall Cemetery. It is the resting place for soldiers from Winchester and other states who gave their lives for the South, while fighting to defend Winchester.

With the passing of time, the sword that Major Jones carried into battle found a home in the Stonewall Jackson's Headquarters Museum on Braddock Street in Winchester. Jackson used the home of Lieutenant Colonel Lewis T. Moore for his headquarters during the winter of 1861–62. Colonel Moore was with the Fourth Virginia. Today, the museum is one of the finest of its kind in the country. It stands as a tribute to Jackson and those who followed him into battle.

For years, Jones's sword leaned in a corner on the second floor with several other swords. The sword of Major Frank Jones is now the only

Thomas "Stonewall" Jackson used this house on Braddock Street as his headquarters during the winter of 1861–62. Now a museum, it is open daily from April through October.

sword in a showcase under lock and key. It seems that, on a daily basis, the staff at the museum heard a sword fall and hit the floor with a clanging crash. This was followed by the sound of a sword being dragged across the floor. When a member of the staff looked into the matter, the sword of Major Jones was on the floor somewhere between the corner and the top of the stairs.

"It was always Jones's sword," said the gentleman who managed the museum at that time.

> *Every afternoon, we'd hear the sword fall and then hear it being dragged across the floor.*
>
> *There was never anyone upstairs when it happened and it only happened when there were no visitors in the museum. Sometimes, we'd find the sword at the top of the stairs. Other times, it would be somewhere between the corner and the top of the stairs. It was never in the same place.*
>
> *It was scary, but it happened every day and was starting to bother the volunteers. I finally put it in the showcase. That stopped it from falling.*
>
> *I think it was Major Jones—and he wanted his sword back.*

Our lady with "the gift" agrees. She says that it is Major Jones and he does want his sword. She says that spirits, at times, will try to reclaim an object that was very dear to them in life.

There is another interesting phenomenon in the museum. Every afternoon, there is a strong smell of pipe tobacco in the room on the first floor that Jackson used as his office. So strong is the smell that it carries throughout the entire building. The burning pipe tobacco can be smelled by staff and visitors alike.

Jackson did not use tobacco, nor did he allow it to be used in his presence. Our "gifted" friend says the pipe tobacco smell is coming from a member of Jackson's staff who is trying to finish his bowl of tobacco before the general returns.

Stonewall Cemetery

The ladies of the South refused to allow their dead to lie in lonesome graves. After the war, groups were formed to create proper burial grounds. In Winchester, a group of women started a movement to bring all the fallen who had fought around the town together in one site.

A portion of Mount Hebron Cemetery was donated and the Stonewall Cemetery was created. Confederates from thirteen states, including one from Delaware, are buried in the Stonewall Cemetery. Only twenty from Arkansas do not have a state monument to mark their resting place.

In the middle of the Stonewall Cemetery stands an impressive monument under which anonymous Confederates are buried. On the north side of the monument is written,

Who they were, none know: What they were, all know.

On the south side is written,

Erected A.D. 1879, by the people of the South, to the 829 Unknown Confederate dead who lie beneath this mound: in grateful remembrance of their heroic virtues, and that their example of unstinted devotion to duty and country may never be forgotten.

Now we come to an interesting question: Are those 829 Confederates truly at rest?

Perhaps they are not.

Across Woodstock Lane is the National Cemetery where Union soldiers who died fighting around Winchester are buried. Only a narrow lane separates the two cemeteries. Yet, at night, a strange thing is known to happen. Just past sundown, people driving or walking along Woodstock

This large monument, erected in 1879 by the people of the South, is dedicated to 829 unknown Confederates.

Lane will see eerie shapes rise from the Confederate Unknown mound and move slowly north toward the National Cemetery. The forms are gray in color and ragged looking. Yet they step like soldiers.

The brave at heart who glance north will see darker colored shapes climbing the stone wall that surrounds the National Cemetery. The two groups appear to advance toward each other. For those who continue watching, an unusual thing happens. When the groups meet, there is no fighting, only a clasping of hands and friendly slaps on the back.

"It happens all the time," said a man with a very unusual gift.

I know most people see it during dusk, but I can see it happening all the time.

They once were enemies; now they are comrades. They are telling war stories and wondering what it was all about. They don't hate each other, they never did. It's almost as though they are forgiving their enemies.

It's a very moving scene. Actually, they are telling each other they would rather be comrades than enemies. It was something they had to do, fight for what they believed.

They wish everyone could see them and hear what they are saying. They feel it is their mission to promote peace.

It's a moving and beautiful thing. They can't understand why people are still fighting. They will not have peace until there are no wars.

I've tried to help them to cross over, but they intend to stay here until the world knows peace.

While walking through the cemetery just before it closes, one is overwhelmed with a strange, chilling feeling. It's a feeling that causes most to leave the Stonewall Cemetery very quickly.

Handley Library

The Handley Library is perhaps the most impressive building in Winchester. It houses one of the finest archives found anywhere. The library and two public schools were built with money left to the City of Winchester by Judge John Handley, of Scranton, Pennsylvania. Today, Winchester's Handley High School boasts that it is the only privately endowed public school in the nation.

Why did the judge leave his money to the City of Winchester?

No one really knows. Judge Handley wanted to be buried in the Stonewall Cemetery, but he was not eligible. As a visiting Yankee, he didn't meet the criteria established by the Stonewall Cemetery organizers. However, Winchester did allow the judge to be buried across the lane from the Stonewall Cemetery, about thirty yards away. Every May, Judge Handley is remembered when schoolchildren lay flowers on his grave.

There are those who do not believe Handley is at rest in his grave. At times, late in the afternoon, someone walking past the library will glance at the round windows in the rotunda to see the face of a man. Everyone describes the man as having a "drooping mustache." Library employees often see a very large man with a mustache and a long frock coat walking up the spiral stairs to the rotunda. No one other than the staff has ever reported seeing the man on the stairs.

It's interesting to note that the man sports a frock coat. That places the wearer back into the 1800s. Handley, being a judge, likely wore such a coat. Also, pictures of the judge show him with a long, drooping mustache. "I know it's Judge Handley," said one employee. "I can feel him. Who else could it be?"

Indeed, who else could it be?

A Ghostly Trip Through the Past

The Handley Library, built in 1908, is an excellent example of the exuberant Beaux Arts style of architecture. The Stewart Bell Jr. Archives, located on the lower floor of the library, has an excellent reputation with genealogists and historians. It houses an extensive collection of materials on people, places and events of the Lower Shenandoah Valley from 1732 to the present.

Other Spirits

There are other spirits in Winchester who, to date, have not been investigated. There's the small lady who roams the second and third floors of the old Lovett building. She is never seen on the first floor but always on the second and third. No one knows who she is. Perhaps someone will investigate.

Across Loudoun Street at Brewbaker's Bar and Grill, a young woman is seen sitting beside the fireplace. Again, no one knows who she is or why she is sitting there. On Fairmont Avenue, there is a house where a man is seen on the stairs. Then he walks into the wall. Who is he, and why does he walk through the wall?

In the basement of a house on South Braddock Street, shackles used to keep slaves from escaping are still bolted into the walls. Also, there is the voice of a slave speaking to her mistress.

These spirits and many more beg investigation. Ah, the stories that our historic, old buildings can tell...

Conclusion

S o...you have dared to read about the dark side of Winchester. If you were of a doubting mind, have you changed your beliefs regarding the spirit world? Yes? No? Are you musing over the possibility that ghosts do really exist?

Perhaps what you have just read is troubling to your mind. If we have troubled you, we are truly sorry. If your mind has not changed, that is all right as well.

We do hope you enjoyed learning about our heritage and historic Winchester.

For us, yes, we do believe in the spirit world. After all, that is all it can be. That is all it ever will be. Remember, no one has gone to their world and come back to tell us about it...

Please visit us at
www.historypress.net

www.ingramcontent.com/pod-product-compliance
Lightning Source LLC
Chambersburg PA
CBHW060814100426
42813CB00004B/1074